Praise for *The Lazy Teacher's Handbook*

If being lazy could be seen as an accolade, then the author of this book would deserve one. Jim Smith has brought laziness to a new level. The book explains how teachers can enjoy their responsibility by helping the learners to realise that they have to share the work...and in doing so they will enjoy it and find it fulfilling.

Of course, 'lazy' is a misnomer; the book oozes professionalism and rigour and it does so with a confidence that will encourage teachers to think again about their classroom practice. It is about the highest quality learning brought about by taking a different slant on how the teacher needs to perform. It is full of the practical explanations of how to make things work and sensible explanations to support classroom organisation. Over the years we have enjoyed seeing cooks, gardeners and DIY experts let us into their trade secrets. This book does it for teachers.

Mick Waters, Professor of Education,
President of the Curriculum Foundation

There are many books on the market which offer a compendium of fun and funky ideas for teachers anxious to engage their students more actively in their classes. However I've not encountered many to match this one for writing style (lucid, easy and entertaining, much in the manner of his mentor Ian Gilbert), organisation and coherence to a unifying idea – the notion that teachers can and should teach less so that learners learn more.

In offering up his 'Lazy Way' antidote to teacher fatigue and student passivity I'm reminded of John West-Burnham's suspicion that children go to school in order to watch their teachers work. The author of this book sets about combating these tendencies with a series of chapters addressing such themes as lesson outcomes, marking, IT, classroom language, differentiation, SEAL (Social and Emotional Aspects of Learning), the use of teaching assistants, etc, and packing each with a pot-pourri of ideas for practical and learner-led classroom activities. Few of these activities

are original, although many have been given creative twists. On the contrary, in keeping with the 'Lazy Way,' the author has unashamedly pinched and synthesised ideas from a rich panoply of sources – his past and present colleagues, courses he's attended, books he's read (Sue Cowley's oeuvre is an apparent influence) and – perhaps most significantly and congruently – students he's taught. The overall product is a delight and will be richly welcomed by teachers seeking to claim back their lives in the face of relentless demands imposed by national diktat, institutional expectations, student and parental expectations, and their own inner voices of guilt and self-denial.

Although this book orients itself deliberately towards the hard-pressed classroom practitioner and therefore wears its research base lightly, there is very little within it that doesn't have a distinguished academic pedigree as a buttress – not least a strong emphasis on reflective, metacognitive and meta-learning tasks which put the learner in control of his or her own learning development. It will therefore avoid the charge justly levelled at some of its antecedents – that it's not much more than a populist collection of superficially attractive but learning- and evidence-lite tips-for-teachers of the 'Here's another learning style questionnaire' variety.

In summary, this book deserves a place in every staffroom. Place it on the centre table, invite all staff to enjoy it and then, to misquote Auden,

Stop all the bells, disconnect the LCD
Deny the kids a wordsearch with a mental age of three
Dazzle the inspector and with seated bum
Bring on Independence, and let Learning come.

Dr Barry Hymer, Managing Director,
Still Thinking UK Ltd and Visiting Fellow,
Newcastle University's Centre for Learning and Teaching

Jim Smith has produced a lively, humorous and invaluable guide to teaching in *The Lazy Teacher's Handbook*. The crucial point for teachers like me is that you can be a more effective teacher by doing less: less photocopying, less in-depth planning, less fussing about discipline. If you imbibe the essential principles he outlines in the book, you'll find yourself with a great toolkit of pupil-proof teaching techniques which will make you enjoy your teaching more and help you get better results. I learnt a lot from the book and would whole-heartedly recommend it to other colleagues.

Francis Gilbert, author I'm A Teacher, Get Me Out Of Here *and* Working The System: How To Get The Best State Education For Your Child, *www.francisgilbert.co.uk*

This is an ideal book for those students and teachers willing to think creatively – outside the box. As an adviser, inspector and a trainee mentor it is always a privilege to observe inspirational teaching – the best of which appears effortless – not so of course. I recall one lesson in particular, a KS2 geography lesson with a mixed age group. I was a few minutes late and missed the remarkably short introduction. The young, petite, soft spoken teacher was almost invisible in the class but the pupils were working so hard, enthused by the tasks, thinking and learning collaboratively. This was no 'lazy teacher' – the activities had been researched and prepared thoroughly. The role of the teacher should be that of a facilitator – and that is the underlying message of this book – 'what if we worked less and they worked more'/'the combination of independent learners and lazy teachers is the outstanding combination that every school should be striving for'.

It is a catalogue of good practice – with emphasis on reflection by the practitioner, minimizing the use of the dreaded worksheets, offering a range of strategies promoting collaborative learning in tune with the individualized, personalized and independent learning agenda and effective classroom management, the effective use of classroom assistants and IT. The strategies are not all new and reference is made to several other publications such as Ian Gilbert's

Little Book of Thunks and Blooms' *Taxonomy* but the catalogue is well set out and is very readable, the most useful being the many strategies offered to improve group work and discussion. It is an effective summary of good practice.

The most progressive sections are the chapters which deal with outcome-led learning and planning. Tips such as – 'don't just wait for the end of the lesson to reflect on outcomes', revisiting the learning outcomes and constant intervention, indeed ensure effective learning, engaging pupils in dialogue about their learning. We have been through the three/four/five part lessons but the 'Lazy lesson structure', stating that a 'lesson is never constrained by a preordained number of parts' and tips such as 'powerful plenaries' and 'the expert deployment of a plenary' provide sound guidance.

In the chapter on marking, the author tells how he trains students 'to be as good at marking' as him. Phrases and activities which enhance students' self-esteem and their motivation provide teacher ammunition. Other useful lists include the word bank for 'outcome words' and no one could disagree with the claim that 'outstanding teaching is all about differentiation'.

The majority of the examples given are from KS3/4 but could be adapted to any age group or subject area and I would certainly recommend this publication to trainees on the Initial Primary Teacher Training course at our University. There is an undercurrent of criticism of PGCE courses for example with regard to effective use of teaching assistants – not so I would hasten to say here at Trinity where we consider ourselves to be progressive, reflecting on current best practice! We certainly would not condone 'laziness' either and the title – although well-meant – could easily be misinterpreted by some of the more laid-back trainees. This is a guide book for enthusiastic and creative teachers.

Marian Thomas, Head of ITET,
Trinity University College Carmarthen

Among the crop of new books aimed at helping teachers think about their teaching, *The Lazy Teacher's Handbook* is clearly written, condenses useful wisdom on how children learn, and offers encouragement.

In order to develop, beginning teachers require encouragement to take risks and practical advice. *The Lazy Teacher's Handbook* is full of interesting ideas.

I shall recommend this book to beginning teachers as an accessible introduction about how to put children at the centre of their practice.

Written in an engaging and down-to-earth style, *The Lazy Teacher's Handbook* is packed full of 'things to try' in lessons, but is also underpinned by a view of teaching and learning that is humane and hopeful.

**John Morgan, Reader in Education,
Institute of Education London and University of Bristol**

THE LAZY TEACHER'S HANDBOOK

How Your Students Learn More When You Teach Less

Jim Smith

Edited by Ian Gilbert

Crown House Publishing Ltd
www.crownhouse.co.uk
www.crownhousepublishing.com

First published by
Crown House Publishing Ltd
Crown Buildings, Bancyfelin, Carmarthen, Wales, SA33 5ND, UK
www.crownhouse.co.uk

and

Crown House Publishing Company LLC
6 Trowbridge Drive, Suite 5, Bethel, CT 06801, USA
www.crownhousepublishing.com

© Jim Smith 2010

Illustrations © Les Evans

'The Lazy Teacher' is a registered trademark.

First published 2010. Reprinted 2010 (three times), 2011 (twice), 2012, 2013.

British Library of Cataloguing-in-Publication Data
A catalogue entry for this book is available
from the British Library.
Print ISBN 978-184590289-6
ePub ISBN: 978-184590409-8
Mobi ISBN: 978-184590408-1

LCCN 2009936661

Printed and bound in the UK by
Henry Ling, Dorchester, Dorset

To Wendy, Henry and Oscar – thank you.
I hope you know why.

Contents

Acknowledgements

It goes without saying that this book is a result of being in education as both a consumer and a supplier. There are simply too many of my former teachers, current colleagues and indeed students who have influenced my thinking to name them all individually. Furthermore every day brings new ideas from different people meaning the list is ever growing. The fear of missing someone out is too great. So to you all, thank you.

I am incredibly lucky to spend some of my time working with Independent Thinking Ltd tapping into the skills, talents and support that can only be provided by such a caring, passionate and in many ways incongruent group of people you could ever wish to meet. Yet somehow, perhaps united by their passion, they all combine together to be this amazing educational inspiration to so many, including me. To you all, thank you.

Achieving success is often about belief. The support of Ian Gilbert, the founder of Independent Thinking, and Caroline Lenton at Crown House Publishing gave me tremendous belief to write a book that would genuinely help others make a difference to how they teach. To you both, thank you.

If my family was to ever run a business, it would be a school. So many of us work or did work in schools almost to the point that Christmas dinner was more like a staff meeting than a celebration! Hence from an early age I have been surrounded by people I now recognise to be outstanding educationalists. My late Gramps, Harold, with his relentless praise and belief in young people (well, certainly when it came to cricket) and my mum, for her willingness to totally ignore the latest initiative and keep learning in practical, mucky and fun ways (meaning she was treated with the utmost respect by students and parents alike). In hindsight I have benefited from two amazing role models who have shaped my beliefs and values. Thank you.

Finally, to my wife Wendy and our gorgeous children Henry and Oscar. To be surrounded by unconditional love, support and encouragement is something very special. It is not so much, thank you; more, I love you.

Foreword

'Last Thursday, dressed like Minnie Mouse and sick with the flu, I sang the Hokey Cokey song to a classroom full of gawking parents and students. As usual, the students just sat there in silence as I sang slightly off-key to myself. And as the song on the CD got to the part, "Put your bottom in", I thought "I'll quit before I bend over in front of this room full of people." I'd reached my limit of humiliating situations I was willing to endure in the name of being a good teacher. So I shut off the CD player mid-song and taught the rest of the lesson from the comfortable position of my chair.'

The above is an on-line blog from an EFL teacher in Japan who has written it from the 'Lazy English Teacher's' point of view. It sums up, I feel, what goes through the mind of so many teachers, this nagging sense that they are working so much harder than the children. And that this can't be right.

Teacher stress is a big issue. According to the online 'Teacher Stress Archive', work-related stress is the biggest health and safety issue in four out of five schools in the UK, leading to health issues including 'anxiety, depression, heart disease, back pain, gastrointestinal disturbances and various minor illnesses'. It even has its own acronym in research circles – TSB or Teacher Stress and Burn Out. (There is an irony in calling it TSB in view of the fact that teachers often find it difficult to say no.)

And that's when you've been teaching for a while. According to an article in *The Independent* a while back, the pressures teachers are under in their first year of teaching, 'are equivalent to someone coming out of medicine and becoming a brain surgeon straight away'.

When I started teaching I remember likening it to being constantly in a business meeting, always this sense of needing to be somewhere else doing something else but not quite being able to get there. What's more, it all kicked off the moment you arrived in the car park. Sometimes I couldn't get the door open for all the students standing there with their wild excuses about why they hadn't done their French homework. Not the long and gentle lead-in to the daily grind that I had when I worked for a local council. Here, people used to tell me that they didn't really do any work until the tea trolley had been round. That was at 10.30 am.

According to research from 1987 on the problem of TSB*, there are two things that can be done. One is to learn how better to deal with stress. In other words, this is the way it is, it's not going to change so how can I ensure I am responding to it in the most healthy and effective way. Rather than reaching for the corkscrew the minute you get back from work it could be a spot of meditation and some visualization techniques. Then the corkscrew.

The other approach is what the researchers call 'direct action'. In other words, addressing the root cause of the stress in the first place. Which brings me back to the teacher who was all Hokey Cokey'ed out.

Without taking away from how serious work stress is, I do wonder how much more teachers can do to help themselves? What if we were able to work less? What if we stopped trying to control everything that happened in our classrooms, all the time? What if we could have the students doing more of the work? What if this was taught from day one as we started our career? What if our aim was to send *them* home exhausted at the end of the day while we were the ones who skipped off to the sweet shop? And what if working in such a way not only helped improve our erstwhile skewed work-life balance but also improved the quality of their learning?

In other words, what if we taught less, but they learned more?

Far from being some distant Nirvana, this is exactly what *The Lazy Teacher's Handbook* is describing, through the words and deeds of Jim Smith, the laziest teacher in town. So much of what goes on

---

*Kyriacou, C, Teacher stress and burnout: An international review, Educational Research. Vol 29(2), Jun 1987, 146-152.

in your working day, from tutor time to testing, setting lesson objectives to setting homework, could be delegated to your students in a way that saves you energy but also involves them in the process of learning in a way that is both motivational and effective when it comes to their own achievement.

And before you think to yourself that you could see yourself doing such a thing with your top set but not that bottom set group you always do battle with, remember, like respect, you get control by giving it. The more you can let them 'take over', the fewer battles you will have. This is something I have seen time and time again with teachers of some very challenging groups.

So, be a professional teacher, be a committed teacher but, in everybody's interest, be a lazy one too and remember, as the Eskimo proverb says, 'If you sweat, you die'.

Ian Gilbert
Dubai
January 2010

Introduction

Have you ever had that niggling worry that the more effort you put into your lessons, the worse things become? Have you ever thought it wrong that you are the one crawling home on your knees at the end of the day whilst the students seem to find a new lease of energy as soon as the bell goes? Does it ever cross your mind how everyone else you know seems to have a life and you don't?

Ever wondered if the hours and hours you spend every day on your job could be time better spent? Ever thought there must be a better way?

Well, the Lazy Teacher is here to help. So, let me put another question to you: Ever wondered what would happen in your classroom if you stopped teaching?

You might be surprised.

Over the last few decades the demands of countless education initiatives from across the whole political spectrum, not to mention the pressures good teachers put on themselves, has seen too much teaching squeezed into our lessons at the expense of learning. In fact, such pressures might just be the reason that students who have been 'boosted' or 'Wave 3 intervened', 'mentored' or 'targeted' are still not progressing quite as we would want. Maybe if we spent a little less time teaching and gave students a little more time to learn, things would be different.

Or, to put it another way, what if we worked less and they worked more?

This is where the Lazy Teacher can help you get more out of your students and at the same time help you to get your life back. More than just a series of tricks, the Lazy Way is something I have put together over years of experience working with all sorts of learners (and teachers) who want their lessons to be different and still get exam success. It was borne out of my frustration with doing a job I love but being slowly killed by it in the process. And as all good psychologists know, if necessity is the mother of invention then frustration is the absent father.

The first time I realised that I needed to review my approach to teaching was towards the end of my first term in the job. In fact, the thought struck me one day as I was waking up, a fact made all the more interesting as I was not actually in bed at the time but in an Indian restaurant. I had gone there to celebrate my new job with several friends and had been overcome by the fatigue of being a teacher. My friends, who all had 'proper' jobs and a chip on their shoulders about how long my holidays were, let me doze, much to the amusement of the other customers and the entire staff of the Star of Bengal.

It was at this point I realised that if I was going to survive in this career then something had to give. And it sure as hell wasn't going to be Friday nights out with my friends.

Although such end-of-term occurrences are now rare it still has to be said that teaching is, quite frankly, exhausting. There really is no other word for it. According to research, the average classroom teacher makes more than 1,500 educational decisions every school day. That's more than four decisions every minute. So, it is hardly surprising that teachers end the day on their knees. Add to that the fact that so much of our 'spare time' is given over to doing the bits of the job we don't have time to do during the school day because we're too busy teaching, and you can wave goodbye to any thoughts of pastimes, hobbies or a social life, let alone having the time to be a half-decent partner or a parent.

So, it didn't take very long into my teaching career before I knew that I had to do something differently. I had to come up with a plan B so I could succeed in this great job without letting the great job take over my life. I needed to find a way to work less but still do the right thing by my students. And then it struck me: there are more of them than me! What if I had them doing more of the work? Why was I the one busting a gut all the time running from the photocopier to the stock cupboard, handing out books and taking in homework as I went? Why was I constantly on the go while they just sat there? It was *their* education after all.

It was at that point, bitten by the twin radioactive spiders of resentment and fatigue, that the Lazy Teacher was born.

Before you start writing letters to *The Guardian*, let's define terms. Can I firstly clarify that I am *not* describing myself as lazy in a 'couldn't care less, take it or leave it, give me my pay cheque and I'm out of here' sort of way. Far from it. I can honestly say that I have never stolen a living from the schools I have worked in. Although the strategies in this book mean that you could, if you wanted to, spend a great deal more time sitting at the front of your class with your feet up and cradling a cup of coffee that is actually hot, this is not what the Lazy Way is all about. I'm the Lazy Teacher not the idle one.

Like so many of us, I am a dedicated and passionate teacher who sees the teacher's job as doing all that is necessary to bring out the best in their students. *But that's just it.* If the teacher does 'all that is necessary' what's left for the students to do? Maybe the more we play the professional fully committed teacher card, the more of a disservice we do our students, never actually giving them the opportunity and the push they need to take control of the learning – their learning – themselves.

Instead of such a disservice, the Lazy Way, as I like to call it, seeks genuinely to raise standards, help students find a love of learning that will last them a lifetime and prevent half our current work-force considering leaving the profession because of stress.

The more you think about it, the more you will agree that being a Lazy Teacher would solve a lot of these problems, and at a fraction of the current educational budget.

When you become a Lazy Teacher, you will employ a series of strategies that put the responsibility of learning directly and consistently onto the students. In doing so they learn to engage with their own learning, and not just in *what* they have learned but in *how* they learned it. In other words, it is not just learning outcomes that are important but the process of learning itself.

In making that switch, you will be freed up to reflect upon – and be critically focused on – the learning, not the teaching. In other words, the Lazy Way is highly professional, highly skilled and something every student should experience as they prepare for a lifetime of learning.

And it's Ofsted-friendly too, especially in light of the fact that nearly every initiative coming from central government at the moment seems to revolve around individualised, personalised and independent learning.

The Lazy Teacher's Handbook is my way of getting over to you that the Lazy Way is your only hope for raising achievement in your classrooms *and* having a life at the same time. So whilst I am happy to share with you as many tips and strategies as I can squeeze into these pages, it is important for you to remember that they are just a starting point. The most important thing is for you to take on board the Lazy Way for yourself and, in doing so, it will start to permeate your own working practices and professional life. When it does, you will be amazed how quickly you start to look at all aspects of your teaching life with fresh new eyes – lazy eyes if you like; eyes that are always on the lookout for ways that you can get students to do the work and benefit the most in the process.

Each chapter in this book is devoted to a different topic covering the full gamut of teacher responsibility, from lazy ways to get the marking done to lazy language that actually helps build self-esteem. I even show you how to get your teaching assistants involved in the whole lazy process. More often than not I avoid a step-by-step account telling you directly how to be lazy as, even in print, this could come across as patronising. Given the simplicity of the ideas (being lazy is not rocket science) I have every confidence that you will be able to take my ideas as a starting point and run with them. Or rather, take these ideas, hand them over to your students and sit back while they do the running.

All of the ideas that follow have a proven track record in helping you become an outstandingly lazy yet outstanding teacher. Some of them have been included because the students have said they made a difference to their learning, some because students said they were fun and some because they were just weird enough to work. In fact many of the ideas were thought up in the first place by the students themselves. What they all have in common is they have the students working more and you working less, putting students right at the heart of learning.

One bit of advice before you start: changing the way you do things in your classroom is a whole lot easier if you remember to engage the students. It seems obvious but it is often forgotten. As Independent Thinking's Ian Gilbert says, 'Do things with them, not to them.' Be open and honest about what you are doing and communicate what their new role is going to be in the classroom. Otherwise it's like starting a new game without telling everyone the rules. It might be fun to start with, but they will soon give up and call it, and you, a failure. So make sure that, at the end of a couple of lessons, you ask for feedback about what parts of the lesson made the students think most, learn most and how they would like their lessons to be in the future. You might be surprised how articulate the students can be.

Like all good learning, the book does not follow a linear path. Pick it up and cherry-pick an idea or systematically work through any chapter then skip to another one. It is designed for short bursts of inspiration to get you thinking and then, importantly, doing.

Your challenge then is to become a Lazy Teacher in your own right. To embrace not only many new strategies and ideas but also to change your whole ethos about what being a committed, professional twenty-first century teacher is all about. After all, you can't lead from the front if you're on your knees under the desk.

Chapter 1

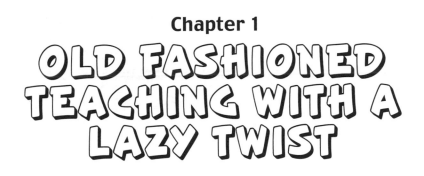

Chapter 1
Old Fashioned Teaching with a Lazy Twist

There are as many different ways to be lazy in the classroom as there are teachers. The Lazy Way does not seek to eliminate that element of diversity, far from it. Across a school there will be a whole range of teaching styles from the more didactic 'traditional' teaching to the weird, wacky 'just call me Jim' approaches. It is what makes schools such a rich and wonderful tapestry of human life and learning, the same task being legitimately addressed in so many different ways.

The Lazy Way is a distillation of many different approaches you might take in your classroom to match what you do to what students need, yet are all linked by one common thread – get the students to do the work. So, while I am happy to advocate many traditional ways of working, such as teacher talk, silent time, group work, use of ICT and the odd trip out of the classroom, all of these should be employed in a way that ensures the students are kept active, thinking and out of trouble.

The big challenge for teachers taking on board the Lazy Way is often dragging themselves away from the safety net that is the scheme of work (or scheme of learning if you've just had an INSET day on the subject). Although this document may be in a shiny new folder ready for the imminent Ofsted inspection, it is often based around thinking and methodology that is decades old. To find out if this is the case may I suggest something I like to call the Photocopier Challenge, an easy and straightforward way of finding out the extent to which you are wasting your own time, let alone letting others waste it for you too. And once you have tested yourself in this way, try the test on your colleagues. You will be amazed at how many heated debates you can start just standing in line at the photocopier. Simply print out the list of questions below which challenge the pedagogical imperatives of your impending actions with the photocopier and stick it on the wall near the machine:

■ Why have I printed paper copies?

■ What types of activity will this lead to?

■ Are these activities to do with learning or filling the time or crowd control or something else?

■ How is the sheet going to be marked?

■ How is the learning going to be assessed?

■ How much of the worksheet do you intend to read to the whole class?

■ Do all students have to start from the beginning?

■ Do all students have to work through to the end?

■ How could it have been done without any photocopying in the first place?

The list could go on, but I am sure you get the idea.

This is not simply an attack on worksheets (although if that's a wordsearch you've just put on the photocopier, it is). What I do attack, however, are the teachers who are continuing to do what they have always done without recognising that both education and the people we teach have changed.

An experienced colleague of mine constantly moans that teachers new to the job are unable to plan a lesson without an interactive whiteboard, a projector and a computer. While he is rightly concerned about the lack of creativity and confidence in those entering the profession, I would suggest that there are a fair few teachers with rather more experience who similarly only feel confident to go into lessons as long as they have the reassuring warmth of a pile of freshly photocopied handouts clutched to their bosom.

As the Lazy Teacher I may well use photocopied material or a movie. I will certainly use ICT and anything else I can get my hands on (although I am probably not alone in thinking ICT has a habit of letting you down when you most need it). But I also know that the success of that lesson is not down to what resources I show up with. Nor will the success of the lesson be down to what I, as the teacher at the front of the class, can pull out of the hat at the last minute.

How do I know this? Because at the heart of the lesson you won't find the PC, the projector, the interactive whiteboard, worksheets or any of the other 'essentials' of a modern classroom. You won't even find a teacher. You will find the students.

That is why the Lazy Way stands up to the Photocopier Challenge.

This chapter highlights four of the most common teaching strategies to be found in classrooms today but gives them the Lazy Way makeover. More evolution than revolution, but a significant change that will make your lessons outstanding in everyone's eyes.

The strategies included here are not meant to be new. Embracing the Lazy Way is often just a subtle shift of focus away from what *you* are going to be doing in a lesson and onto what *they* are going to be doing; in other words a subtle shift from teaching to learning. 'A new twist on an old approach' is how it was once described to me when I was working with a school looking to transform their learning.

A subtle new twist it may be, but never underestimate the determination needed to mobilise even a small shift in embedded traditions. And small though that shift may be, its implications can be seismic.

The combination of independent learners and lazy teachers is *the* outstanding combination that every school should be striving for. It is worth every bit of effort to challenge existing practice in our classrooms and make that small but powerful shift. After all, are we not collectively bound by a moral and professional duty to do *the* best possible job for our children? And that may well have to be the line you use next time you are confronted by a frantic colleague looking for their photocopying.

Four common lazy teaching styles get the lazy makeover

The most common teaching styles I see teachers using and are:

- whole class instruction
- whole class debates and discussions
- group work
- silent work (or more accurately, attempted silent work).

Given a lazy twist these can remain in your repertoire of what you do in your classroom. And remember, these approaches can be blended with ideas and strategies from all the other chapters to make your whole lesson a lazy lesson.

Makeovers for whole-class instruction

Sometimes speaking to the whole class as one is an appropriate way to teach. You just need to be constantly reminding yourself that it is often the students' least preferred way of learning. So knowing that, if you are still going to do it, at least you can give it a Lazy Teacher makeover so you can spend less time doing it and, when you do it, it has genuine impact.

Record your key messages

Many airlines now have abandoned much of their pre-flight safety briefings in favour of a pre-recorded message on a screen. Whilst this is much to the disappointment of those who enjoyed watching a newly qualified air steward fumble with their whistle, safety belt and inflatable jacket, it is perhaps done in this way to have greater impact with the passengers. The same could happen in your classroom. Do you have set routines for entry or exit that could be played via a screen enabling you to concentrate during those precious last moments of the lesson on a student's learning? Imagine never having to settle, dismiss or instruct a class to pack away again. And don't forget, the students love to create the movies for you.

The students will also respond to the use of audio recordings when you want to communicate with the class. A sense of intrigue will waft over your classroom as the students work out it is you reading the poem, offering praise or giving out clues to the challenge they are undertaking – all without moving your lips.

Become unpredictable

There is a sense of inevitability when a teacher assumes the 'talk to the class' position and posture. On many occasions I have felt the energy and sense of anticipation drain from the room as the students become all too aware of what is to follow – a didactic lecture, which if they are 'lucky' may have some PowerPoint slides. So when you do have to talk to the whole class for a period of time (and can I stress once again, it does happen) at least try to disguise that it is about to happen.

So, simply vary where you stand in the room, what you are standing on and even what you are wearing during your talk. Wearing a series of hats or wigs and standing on a milk crate are what you need to get their curiosity juices flowing! If the dressing up box is still in its infancy (although with the number of car boot sales and jumble sales, there really is no excuse) you can still be unpredictable with your accent! Simple? Yes! Silly? Yes! Will the students really listen? Yes!

Explain the importance

When you have the whole class focused on what you are saying, emphasise the importance of what you are saying and that you will not be able to repeat it. On this occasion you should probably avoid the obvious cliché of putting on your best French accent and stating, 'I shall say this only once', but their innate desire not to miss out or give their peers an advantage by not listening properly is a strong factor in your favour.

Delegate to students

Ask students in advance to help you deliver key bits of the lesson by arranging 'guest experts' to address the class and impress their mates. And, of course, your students may well wish to use some of the variations described above. Who said the milk crate, dressing up box and silly voices were just for you?

Makeovers for whole–class debates and discussion

Done badly, whole-class debate and discussion can often be the undoing of the learning in your lesson. It is a major reason why you might find Ofsted downgrading your overall lesson judgement. Why? Too many teachers are paraphrasing student answers then adding in an anecdotal by-line for good measure meaning the majority of the students disengage with a crucial part of the learning.

Why the vast majority of teachers feel compelled to repeat and add something to every response they receive is beyond me. You have a whole class of students who should be asked to comment on what has just been said. The Lazy Way will give you the tools to enable everyone in your class to speak, listen and offer opinion, as well as giving your voice and the students' ears a well-earned rest.

Sweeping

This technique is designed to keep the whole class together but also enables you to make sure everyone has an equal opportunity to speak uninterrupted and without challenge. You will also develop self-assured students who want to share their views, confident in the fact that the debate is structured and will not be overshadowed by the person who can shout the loudest (and that includes the teacher).

Get your group seated in a circle with everyone facing inwards. This can be on chairs or on the floor. Choose a student to start and tell the group you will be moving round in a clockwise direction asking each person to speak. There is no interruption or feedback from anyone during the sweep round the circle, including you. This is the Lazy Way, remember. Allow students to pass without saying anything in order that they have more thinking time (it is a subtle form of differentiation after all). Yet always come back to those students so you model inclusion and an expectation that everyone contributes in your lesson.

Sweeping works really well with a range of responses from group warm-ups, where it might be a short response to a fun question such as 'If you were a car, what type of car would you be and why?' to a more emotive question such as, 'Do you believe testing chemicals on animals is cruel?' where you might be trying to engage lots of people without letting the deeper debate start too early.

Circle time feedback

This builds on the sweeping strategy in Makeover 1 and is used to offer a clear, controlled structure for debate. What is lazy about it? The students run it.

Before you start, communicate a maximum time limit that anyone can speak for. Remember, even thirty seconds is actually quite a long time, so don't be too ambitious.

Decide as a group what silent gesture you are going to make if you wish to add to the debate (a raised hand or leg will normally do the trick). When a student has finished speaking (and ideally not before), the student who has spoken looks to see if anyone is making the agreed silent gesture and invites them to speak. You avoid personal debates by putting a rule in place that you cannot hand back to the person who has just spoken and also you should have a student in charge of making sure time limits are adhered to. If a student overruns their time limit they are excluded from the debate.

Ask the students to devise a range of signals that indicate not only that they want to speak, but whether they agree or disagree with the comments being made – for example, right hand raised for agree, left hand raised disagree.

Envoying

Using small groups is an effective way to handle a discussion so that, to use mobile phone jargon, everyone can get more 'airtime'. However, the downside to such an approach is that it can lead to off-task behaviour as the small group knows it is very hard for you to hear what is being said and see what is being done. Your students' acting skills easily extend to disguising a conversation about the weekend whilst picking away at the furniture as an in depth discussion on the causes of the First World War. This is where you, the newly converted Lazy Teacher, can use the students' natural instinct and desire to win to great effect. And rather than wait too long, five minutes is plenty before you unleash this strategy.

Send one member (to be known as the 'envoy') from their group to visit another group. The envoy is there with two missions: (1) to listen to the group's ideas so he can report back to his own group and (2) to share his own group's ideas with his hosts. This is a very lazy way of making sure everyone remains engaged with the task and hears other viewpoints without you wrestling for silence with the class.

Think–Pair–Square–Share

This strategy enables you to quickly engage the whole class in a range of skills without losing any time moving furniture or formulating groups. Think–Pair–Square–Share is a series of steps that involve no preparation from you, yet will make the students move through the stages of individual work, paired work and group work before feeding back to the whole class with effortless ease.

Think: The students spend time in silence writing or thinking about their own ideas.

Pair: Students turn to the person next to them to discuss their ideas with a partner.

Square: Two pairs work together to complete the task of drawing out the quality responses from the quantity the first two phases have thrown up. They also elect who will be speaking. This stage is crucial for extracting the high level explanation behind why an answer was chosen.

Share: A nominated student feeds back to the whole class the ideas that have been generated.

This strategy is at its best when you want to turn quantity of ideas into quality of ideas. The first two phases concentrate on quantity, the last two on quality. Think–Pair–Square–Share is so much more engaging for the students and lazy for you, that never again should you be standing at the front trying to remember whether or not it is politically correct to say, 'Let's brainstorm some ideas.'

The quality stage is in the sharing. Prior to sharing, ask each group to select and justify a restricted number from their list so that they work on giving explanations and justifications. It is a lazy way of tricking them into some very good explanative reasoning.

Thinking line–up

This is the ultimate way to set up lots of opportunities for students to discuss their views with others in the class. What's more there is no way you can join in, meaning you have to be lazy!

Ask the students to generate a 'thinking continuum', which is a single line of students standing in an order which reflects their varying thoughts about a statement. A good one to get going could be, 'Should the government make school uniform compulsory in all schools?' or 'Should the government allow animal testing if it provided a cure for cancer?' At one end of the line you have 'totally agree' and at the other end 'totally disagree'. Students can then begin to work out where they should stand, checking the views of those on their right and left to make sure they are in the correct place.

Once you have done that (and do not rush this stage as it is quite challenging) you can begin to have fun with the line using the following Lazy Way variations.

Bend my viewpoint

Once you have your line formed, bend it in half so the two opposing ends are opposite each other to form a tunnel. Students can then have a discussion about the views held by the person opposite them. After a few minutes, rotate the line randomly so all students get to discuss their views with someone who was furthest away from their position in the continuum.

Group it

Once the line is formed go along and divide the line into groups of three. This way you put students with similar viewpoints together. They then have an opportunity to work on a presentation that would explain why they held their views as well as questioning the views held by others.

A variation on this would be to go down the line choosing every fifth person and put them in a group together to discuss their different viewpoints.

At the end of the discussion allow time to ask the class to re-form the thinking continuum. The students can then see who has moved their position and reflect on why they have – or have not – moved.

Makeovers for group work

Group work, or collaborative learning to give it an upgrade, is increasingly important in lessons. When delivered effectively, group work really does enhance independent learning skills. When delivered badly the resulting chaos may leave you to question the wisdom of your career choice. And the phrasing of those last two sentences is deliberate. Group work is something the lazy teacher delivers, yet the students have total control over at all times.

What follows are five makeovers that can help you to avoid the many pitfalls of group work and instead allow you to take a step back and wallow in the seriously lazy lesson going on in front of you. After all, it is group work and you don't have a group so how can you be doing the work?

Group formation

Always vary how groups are chosen. Be it teacher choice, student choice, gender or skills, it doesn't really matter as long as you are clearly seen to be choosing the groups with a rationale that you share with the students. Sharing of the rationale is important as you are communicating that you expect the newly formed groups to be successful. Yet what I often hear when groups are set up is comments like, 'I hope this will work, but I am not sure it will with you lot working together!' As a rallying call it is hardly a mandate for success. It might be a throwaway comment on your part but what if, as a student, you were hearing this message all the time?

Once the group is formed outline how much time the group has using the following formula:

People x Time = Number of hours to work

If you have a group of four students working for a sixty minute lesson, this equates to four hours of time. Ask the students what they would expect an individual to produce in four hours. You can then use this formula to set the expectation for the group and what they should aim to achieve. Then, instead of running around trying to cajole the students, just refer them to your agreed four hour expectation.

Use of furniture

Insist that the students move the furniture to reflect the number of people in the group. The Lazy Teacher is always looking for an opportunity to question students about the process of learning, and furniture is often missed as an opportunity to stimulate that discussion. Can a group of five really work effectively huddled around a single table or in a long line?

Before any furniture is moved make it clear that the group will put all furniture back at the end of the session. Not only will this reduce any unnecessary rearranging, it will also mean you are not playing catch-up with your expectations later in the lesson.

Task

Lazy Teaching relies on the students beginning to develop skills in the process of learning and understanding which of these newly acquired skills to deploy with each new challenge. To make sure you reflect the importance of these skills, use assessment criteria that cover knowledge and skills. To paraphrase my Independent Thinking colleague Will Ryan, 'Assess what you value. Value what you assess.'

Furthermore, if your students are aware that you will be awarding equal marks to the process (possibly more in the early stages) it reduces the likelihood of one person doing all the work whilst the others sit back and discuss the weekend's big football clash.

Allocate roles

After many lost lunchtimes either setting up or clearing up from group work, I vowed to do it differently. The next time you have planned group work, allocate these five different roles to the students:

■ Facilitator – keeps things moving and records what is happening, which is important if the group work is not one continuous time slot

■ Time keeper – the team clock

■ Resource manager – gathers and returns the resources to and from one designated table

■ Quality checker – keeps teams on-task

■ Team rep – represents the team at 'emergency meetings'.

You can mix and match these roles according to numbers in the group, even create new ones, but the key is to give them a focus over and above the task.

With the roles allocated and in place, you now have a whole range of lazy strategies up your sleeve to make sure your students are in charge so everyone gets to lunch on time. Try the following ideas to make sure you get the most out of the roles.

Facilitator

Ask them for a report that summarises the progress made and what the group's next steps will be at the end of every lesson. This can then be given back to the group at the start of the next lesson to help them to start work straight away. The report should be in any format that gets the information across: text, e-mail, movie/audio clip and handwritten all do the job.

Time keeper

Simply charge them with getting the group to finish on time. And that includes all the packing up and getting the room as you want it. It means you are not bellowing, 'There are five minutes to go and will everyone please look at the clock.'

Resource manager

Make it clear to them from the start that they are the only students allowed to collect resources and they are personally responsible for the safe return of all resources. You then avoid the whole class devouring your annual supply of glue, coloured paper and pens like a plague of locusts. Even better than that, the guilty culprit who lost the missing glue stick lid is narrowed down from your whole class to a handful of resource managers. And when your resource managers realise that they will be the ones staying behind, not their mates, they go hunting for that missing lid as if their lunchtime depended on it. Which it does.

Quality checker

The excitement and creativity that effective group work can generate means there is often the temptation on the student's part to drift away from the success criteria you set. Triple-mounting a handwritten title may be pretty but is unlikely to score the group many marks from the success criteria. Having a quality checker means you know there is a constant thread of someone making sure the work that is going on is relevant and valid.

Team rep

These are the people you can summon if you want to drip-feed information without stopping the whole group from working. Call the team reps together to give them any messages for the whole class. It then becomes the team rep's responsibility to deliver that to their team and check that their team understands it. Why would you want to keep stopping the whole class and interrupting their learning?

Always rotate the roles when you start a new task so people do not become stereotyped. It is important that, over the course of a year, your students get to experience all the different roles and gain a greater understanding that effective group work is not about being with the student who will do all the work for you.

Resources

Let's be honest, there is only so much you can do with sheets of sugar paper and grey and orange pens (the only colours that never seem to run out or go missing). So use resources that are a bit different and make a clear expectation that students use them in a different way.

The following will keep your resource manager (see Makeover 4 above) on their toes, as well as promoting some interesting strategic discussion in the groups.

That's your lot

There will be occasions when you want the groups to focus on the knowledge and the process over and above the finished product. By giving all groups equal but finite resources – such as three sheets of A4 paper, a pen, a pair of scissors, an empty yoghurt pot and 50 cm of Sellotape – you will really focus the group on the process rather than the resources. Experience tells me that the quality of the finished product is rarely proportionate to the amount of paper used.

Choose your lot

If you want to add another layer to the skills being used by your students without any extra work for yourself, vary what resources each group has access to, either by asking them to choose five different resources from the table or pre-packaging different resource bags.

Going, going, gone

You can promote planning as a skill by limiting the number of important resources to less than the number of groups and running a booking sheet for when groups can use them. For example, a good easy one to start with is scissors or glue. There are creative ways around this little challenge, as your students will soon demonstrate. If we value creativity as a skill, we have to offer opportunities to develop this skill. There is no point handing everything to your students on a plate and expecting them to become creative. Limiting their resources may be just the creative challenge your students need.

You have to use a ...

... plant pot in your presentation of population dynamics. Or a bath toy in your presentation on the essential dietary requirements to remain fit and healthy. Occasionally call in your resource managers and hand them an unusual item that has to be built into their group's work. Dealing with unusual changes to the schedule is all part of the world of work. So they might as well start preparing for it now.

'Houston, we have a problem ...'

For the ultimate attempt to foster creativity and enterprise you can issue the resource managers with bags of random resources that you have collected, as well as consumables. Remember to stipulate which ones you might want back unscathed as you will want to use your favourite resources time and time again.

Done the Lazy Way, you will find these subtle changes will revolutionise the way you and your students see group work. You will know you have cracked it when your students arrive, set themselves up and start working without you saying a word. Your students will even chastise latecomers, those not contributing and anyone who is absent, meaning that the students take on behaviour management without even knowing it. It does not come much more lazy than that.

A makeover for silent work

Having the opportunity to work in silence should be built in to the repertoire of what you offer students on a regular basis. It is the perfect opportunity for students to work on their own and genuinely begin to explore aspects of independent learning. However, there are a few points to bear in mind.

- Avoid silent work becoming associated with one form of work by varying the type of task you complete in silence.

- Never use silent work as a punishment as it is valuable way of working, not a consequence of poor behaviour.

- Establish how long you are going to be silent for and make it clear to your class that you do want that amount of time spent in silence and will reset the clock if people talk. After a couple of false starts you will soon get the length of silent working that you want. (I know, after all, it worked for me as a supply teacher.)

- Have strategies to help those who may become stuck or want to talk, for example, doodle pads or other tasks they can do.

- Model working in the silent time as well. If students see you are busy they are less inclined to ask you for help and you have a clear, legitimate purpose for wanting a period of time where you can get on and do! Additionally, do we really want to be patrolling our classrooms making sure everyone is obeying the silent rule? It is hardly conducive to building group rapport.

The reason I introduce you to the four teaching styles above is simply because I feel they are the most common in our classrooms and in our schemes of work. There are others but I think these five make a good start as you begin to embrace the Lazy Way.

If you're not sure where to start you could always – and you should already be picking up a theme here – ask the students. They are on the receiving end of your dominant teaching style most of the time so they should know. In fact, make a game of it and write down what you think they will say and put it in an envelope prior to asking them. How confident are you that the way you perceive your teaching will be the same as they perceive it? Perhaps it doesn't matter. But it should in six weeks time when you survey them again.

Chapter 2

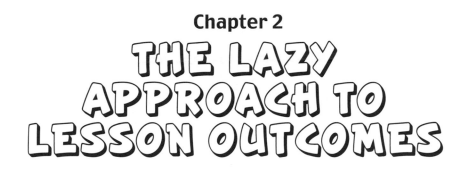

THE LAZY APPROACH TO LESSON OUTCOMES

Chapter 2
The Lazy Approach to Lesson Outcomes

Objective, focus, purpose, intention, goal, target, aim, WIIFM (what's in it for me) and WALT (we are learning to) are all ways of describing and dressing up what I will call the lesson outcome – the crucial statement at the start of the lesson which describes what it is we want out of the learning experience. For the Lazy Teacher, they are crucial and not just because the government tells us things like this:

> Learning outcomes are an integral part of the planning and delivery of effective lessons.
>
> *Creating A Progress Culture*, Secondary National Strategies (London: DCSF, 2007), p. 13

How the Lazy Teacher would interpret their importance would be best summarised by the fact that I believe outcome-led learning is the bedrock of the Lazy Way as well as a method of ensuring our students develop skills that will equip them for the twenty-first century.

It is important, at this stage, that we clarify exactly what an 'outcome' is, or at least how to define it.

A learning outcome is the clear communication of what students are expected to be able to do in order to complete the task successfully. This is not restricted to knowledge as it may also include behaviours. Put another way, it is what is going to happen in your lesson and, should any of the students drift off and need reminding, it is there for them to look at and remind themselves what they are supposed to be doing.

There are three main reasons why learning outcomes are so crucial to the Lazy Way:

1.   It enhances independent learning by identifying which skills are to be used (to explain, to justify, to create). This enables students to develop both curricular and cross-curricular links in their learning skills. Realising that they need one set of skills to be a learner – not ten different sets of skills to be a mathematician, a linguist and a biologist – is the first step in developing independent learning.

2.   An outcome acts as the basis of the highly effective multi-plenary approach. This is where you can ask the students to reflect on what it is they are doing and how it is helping them to achieve their goal during various stages of the 'learning loops' cycle.

3.   A clear outcome enables students to design *for themselves* both the learning process and the means by which they are going to show what they have learned. Truly lazy, but just the way to showcase what wonderful independent learners your teaching ethos has created.

Highlighting specific outcomes does not mean you are blind to other great outcomes that spring up unexpectedly or inadvertently during the lesson. On the contrary, being lazy means you are always alert to great ideas and powerful learning that, without any planning on your behalf, just sort of happens.

This chapter splits the ideas for the lazy approach to lesson outcomes into three sections:

■ five rules to get the best from outcomes – the Lazy Way

■ a handy list of outcome-related words to help start the lesson

■ and a number of simple ideas for starting and ending your lesson.

Ultimately, the clear goal is to make students feed back and talk about outcomes as part of their everyday language in the classroom. It is an incredibly powerful moment when a student stops mid-sentence, the penny drops and they finally realise that they do have the skills to evaluate, explain or analyse. Even better when another penny drops and they realise these are the very same skills they can use or do use in other subjects.

The five rules for using outcomes – the Lazy Way

There are some clear principles about the language of outcomes.

1. **Use student–friendly language**

   Never assume that the pupils understand the language used in the outcome. You are the one with postgraduate qualifications, not them. Therefore avoid overly complex terms and try to build a bank of language that you can repeat so students become aware of the learning process for different key words. 'Explain' is a skill that is the same in any subject, not just yours.

2. **Don't just present a series of tasks**

   Outcomes should require a way in for the learner. This is very hard if outcomes are written as a tick-list of activities or tasks to complete, as these examples show:

   Draw the river system.

   Answer questions 1–10.

   Read and make notes about the discovery of the coping saw.

   Rewritten they could easily read:

   To describe the features and processes of the river system.

   To provide evidence that you can divide by 100.

To identify the significant developments in the creation of the coping saw.

And presented in this way even the creation of the coping saw lesson has more appeal as you are subliminally saying to your well-trained learners, 'Skim read the article looking for significant events and when you have chosen and explained your three points you will have cracked it. Right let's go!'

And if outcomes can work their magic as effectively as that on the coping saw lesson, just think what they could do for your lesson plans.

3. Don't give the game away

Ever had a good book ruined by someone who tells you the ending? For curious minds, a poorly constructed outcome can have the same effect. For example, 'Be able to explain that things dissolve faster in hot liquids rather than cold' rather undermines the need to be in the classroom for the next fifty minutes even if you did have a whizz-bang practical lined up.

4. Don't just wait for the end of the lesson to reflect on outcomes

As we discuss in Chapter 3, outcomes are to be revisited, revised, explored and assessed against a range of different criteria throughout the whole lesson, not just at the end. In doing so, you will train your group to work for longer without any additional input from yourself, as well as ensuring that all-important joint ownership of the outcomes.

5. Mix knowledge and behaviours

Outcomes can include knowledge and/or behaviours. This is especially useful as you can link the two key components to an effective lesson in one go. For example:

To discuss ideas for a new school uniform using the 'no shouting out' rule.

To create a new bird feeder within our group using the *Effective Groupwork Handbook*.

In doing so, you begin to subliminally model the importance of behaviour for learning without having to regurgitate a whole national strategy and series of workshops.

The Lazy Teacher's really useful 'outcome words' word bank

The use of your 'command word' is crucial in developing an outcome, as it offers an opportunity for students to pick up on learning patterns across different subjects. This word bank contains some useful ones you could use across the school to keep outcomes relevant, purposeful and engaging. I tried to come up with an A to Z list but my laziness got the better of me. If anyone can come up with anything for K, Q, U, X, Y or Z let me know, won't you? And 'x-amine' doesn't count.

A	C	D	Differentiate	Extrapolate
Adapt	Calculate	Decide	Discriminate	F
Analogy	Clarify	Decipher	Distinguish	Formulate
Apply	Classify	Decode	Divide	G
Appraise	Combine	Deduce	Draw	Generalise
Argue	Compare	Defend	E	H
Arrange	Compose	Define	Employ	Hypothesise
Assess	Conclude	Demonstrate	Evaluate	I
Assumption	Consider	Describe	Evidence	Identify
B	Construct	Design	Examine	Illustrate
Believe	Contrast	Determine	Experience	Imagine
Break down	Convert	Develop	Experiment	Implement
		Devise	Explain	Improve

Infer	Match	R	Separate	W
Integrate	Model	Rank	Sequence	Write
Interpret	Modify	Reason	Solve	
Interrelate	N	Recall	Sort	
J	Name	Recognise	Speculate	
Judge	Negotiate	Recommend	State	
Justify	O	Reconstruct	Summarise	
L	Order	Record	T	
Label	Organise	Refine	Tabulate	
Link	P	Reflect	Transfer	
List	Paraphrase	Relate	Transform	
Locate	Plan	Reorganise	Translate	
Logically	Predict	S	V	
M	Prioritise	Scan	Validate	
Make connections	Provide evidence	Select	Visualise	

Lazy Ways to celebrate outcomes

There is no shortage of books and websites dedicated to starter and plenary style activities. For the Lazy Teacher, therefore, it is a case of selecting those that complement the Lazy Way. Part of this will mean that you limit working one-to-one in your starters. From the very beginning, push the responsibility onto the students. It is they that need starting, not you.

Random around-the-room questions

A pupil chooses a number and counts that number of people around the room before asking the identified pupil a question related to the outcome. This can also be done Derren Brown-style by the students randomly throwing a soft and catchable object to someone else in the group who then has to answer.

Freeze-frame or mime exercises

After the class has discussed the outcome of the lesson, and what it will take to succeed, selected students create a freeze-frame or short mime of what learning strategy they are going to use to meet the outcome. You might see listening, questioning, mind mapping or a whole variety of skills being modelled. Other students can guess what is happening. This activity works equally well at the end of a learning cycle when you can rephrase the question and ask, 'What learning strategy did you find most useful?' A discussion about what they thought would be useful and what actually was useful is often fascinating.

Stop the clock

Selected pupils present an aspect of their work to the class, but the teacher 'stops the clock' at random times to ask others in the class a question about the presentation (make sure you vary the questions to cover process and content). If you want to take it to the next level, you can stop the clock, then ask a student to ask a

question that another student answers. This is a great way to improve student attentiveness and feedback, whilst avoiding the need for teacher to feed back a comment all of the time.

Hot seat

A pupil sits in the 'hot seat' as an expert or assumes a character and the rest of the class asks questions of that person. No need to restrict experts or characters to humans. One of my favourite lessons of last year was seeing a KS3 English class interrogate 'Mr Wolf' (who was being played by a group of students) about a suspicious house fire and the whereabouts of a certain number of missing little pigs. The class were totally enthralled and the questioning skills second to none.

Sentence summary

Each pupil writes a sentence that summarises the lesson, their learning and the outcome, then shares it with a partner, small group or the class. Add a further frisson to this by asking for a number between one and fifteen which will determine the number of words in the sentence, or a letter between A and Z which will determine the letter to be used for alliterative purposes. If your class is really up for it, why not combine both, 'Eleven words that start with "G" that capture your learning in this lesson, please class!'

Skills dictionaries

Pupils write down the key actions and skills they have used in the lesson to help them achieve their outcomes. These are all collected in the back of the learning planner or rough book. When students are reviewing the progress they have made or want some help as to how to solve a problem or issue, they can refer back to this list to find out what they did last time.

Envoys

A pupils moves as an 'envoy' from their own group to the next group to explain a key idea or present some findings, be it in written, verbal or even dramatic form. They can then return to their own group to share what they have learnt.

The X Factor

A shameless link to popular culture to help sell the concept to your students (but be warned: before they get too excited it has nothing to do with the TV show!). Ask your pupils to identify three ways in which what they have learnt in the lesson, be it a skill or knowledge, might be used *across* other subjects. That is to say the 'Across Factor' (told you!). This forces the students to extend their learning beyond your classroom and link it to what they are doing in other areas of their learning. And by that I mean outside school as well.

The learning journey

Each pupil has to talk for a predetermined amount of time about their learning and the progress they have made towards the learning outcome. The student determines the amount of time, with credit given for both content and timing.

Draw it!

Ask students to draw a simple image in their book to reflect their learning in the lesson. This makes for a refreshing change but also might be training them in another way in which information can be captured.

In hindsight ...

Students have to reflect on their learning and say at least one thing they would like to do differently if they were given the same outcome but could choose a different method. This idea is probably best used with extended challenges, as there is no need to be constantly looking for your own shortcomings in every lesson. That's what line managers are for.

You can see how the use of outcomes in a lazy way can play such a powerful role in developing skills that students need, both at school and in their future careers. It provides a structure and framework within which creativity can thrive yet at the same time providing very clear parameters for assessing both what students achieved in your lesson and, importantly, how they did it. All from a simple single shared sentence at the start of a lesson. How lazy is that?

Chapter 3

STRUCTURING THE LAZY LESSON

Chapter 3
Structuring the Lazy Lesson

'Hey Jim, I really like your tie but I think those shoes were a bad choice. Have you thought about getting some like these, the ones I'm wearing? I think they'd go far better with your hair ...'

Hearing someone tell you how you could improve the structure of your lessons is like being told by someone you don't know very well how you could improve your personal appearance – deeply personal, potentially upsetting but, nonetheless, there might be an element of truth in what is said.

There is a trusted interview question: 'What's the worst someone could say about you, whilst retaining an element of truth?' It is designed to overcome the very personal issue of addressing your faults and weaknesses. It equally applies to your lesson structure, so go on, give it a go: 'What's the worst someone could say about the way your lessons hang together, whilst retaining an element of truth?'

Being a Lazy Teacher doesn't mean doing away with a reliable structure for your lessons. In fact, the Lazy Way needs a very good structure, one that allows your students to engage in the process of learning first and develop a love of medieval kings or oxbow lakes second. Or, put another way, get them to love learning and then you have a chance of getting them to love your subject. Yet creating such a lesson structure is not as onerous as it seems. You just use the same one for all you do. From a launch lesson, to a group work lesson through to a celebration lesson – the Lazy Teacher uses the same structure each time. Anything else just wouldn't be lazy. And if we know what effective learning is, why would we ever want to deviate from it?

Before I share with you Lazy Teacher's multipurpose, dead simple, works every time lazy lesson structure, I feel that a quick history of the lesson structure is in order.

Way back in the mist of time the start of a nationwide frenzy of lesson structure advice began with the launch of the nationally rolled out 'three-part lesson' consisting of starter, activity and plenary (or 'come in, sit down, shut up' as it is more widely known).

However, if lesson structures were cars, this would be the Nissan Cherry of the education world. It has very much had its day and has been left burned out in a beauty spot to be superseded by the bigger, better and much more shiny Vauxhall Vectra four-part lesson.

The four-part lesson replaced activity with the phrases 'guided' and 'independent'. Maybe here can be discerned the green shoots of the Lazy Teaching ethos, a genuine acknowledgement that students really could do some things on their own. However, it wasn't long before the teachers looking down their noses at their meagre three-part lesson colleagues began to voice their discontent with their new improved four-part lessons. For the fourth part was really only a phase called 'independent learning time for the students' and if your students couldn't fill that time, well the teacher just had to talk a bit more before the students copied something off the board.

Nonetheless, some people considered the four-part lesson offered enough of an improvement that vast efforts were put into rewriting schemes of work to fit this format. And for some schools and certain learners, it must be acknowledged, it worked. And still is working. However, the four-part lesson would not win your game of car themed lesson structure Top Trumps. Oh no. There is now evidence that your Vauxhall Vectra has not only been trumped by a Porsche Cayenne five-part lesson but in researching this book I also heard of a Hummer-sized six-part lesson from North Carolina in the United States.

But does super-sizing your lesson structure do anything to promote effective learning? And does it really fit in with the Lazy Teacher ethos we are trying to create – getting you to work less and them to work more?

To be fair, it was this escalating game of pedagogical Top Trumps that led me to developing the Lazy Lesson structure, one that couldn't be beaten because it had no set maximum number of parts to it. Imagine trumping someone's top-of-the-range SUV with a card that happened to feature a jellyfish.

Finally, before I get to my simple lazy lesson structure, a word of advice. I am not advocating that you rewrite all your existing schemes of work because (1) it wouldn't be the lazy thing to do and (2) having reams of documents predicting what you are going to be doing with a group six months hence is not the way to drive up standards. What will improve things all round is a lesson structure that encourages collaborative ownership, independent learning and gives learners the opportunity to review the learning as many times as is necessary until they 'get it'. And that is something that cannot be trumped.

Lazy lesson structure

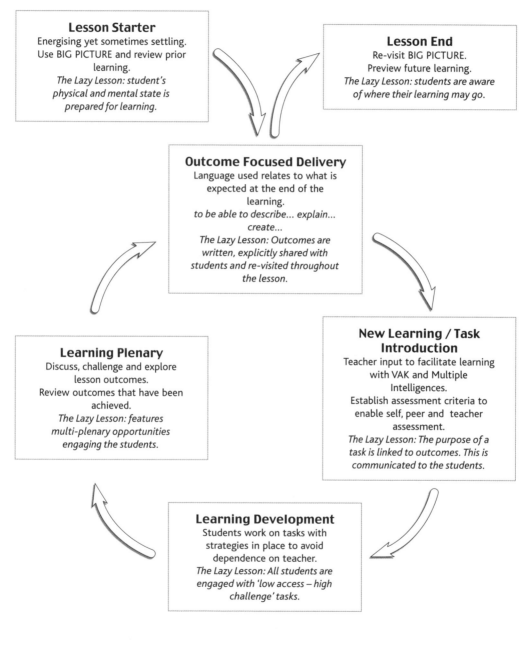

Lesson Starter
Energising yet sometimes settling.
Use BIG PICTURE and review prior learning.
The Lazy Lesson: student's physical and mental state is prepared for learning.

Lesson End
Re-visit BIG PICTURE.
Preview future learning.
The Lazy Lesson: students are aware of where their learning may go.

Outcome Focused Delivery
Language used relates to what is expected at the end of the learning.
to be able to describe... explain... create...
The Lazy Lesson: Outcomes are written, explicitly shared with students and re-visited throughout the lesson.

New Learning / Task Introduction
Teacher input to facilitate learning with VAK and Multiple Intelligences.
Establish assessment criteria to enable self, peer and teacher assessment.
The Lazy Lesson: The purpose of a task is linked to outcomes. This is communicated to the students.

Learning Plenary
Discuss, challenge and explore lesson outcomes.
Review outcomes that have been achieved.
The Lazy Lesson: features multi-plenary opportunities engaging the students.

Learning Development
Students work on tasks with strategies in place to avoid dependence on teacher.
The Lazy Lesson: All students are engaged with 'low access – high challenge' tasks.

The Lazy Teacher's simple but effective lesson structure

The lazy structure is based around a basic 'improvement concept' model designed solely to improve learning in the classroom. In its simplest form, the students should experience it as a straightforward process consisting of an ongoing (not predetermined) series of 'learning loops' that take on board three simple elements: prepare, do and review.

Prepare, do, review

Beware – this simple principle does not mean it is the three-part lesson in disguise! For rather than having a fixed number of parts to a lesson structure, the learning loops in this model are a series of stages that can be repeated as *many times as necessary* in the lesson. A lesson is never constrained by a preordained number of parts and decided by someone behind a desk building an empire far away from a real classroom.

To add further flexibility, another key principle is that learning is *not a linear activity*. Far from it. Learning in the lazy lesson consists of an ongoing series of these loops, some planned, some unplanned, and all dictated by what actually happens in the lesson.

What's more, the amount of time spent on each phase is governed by the nature of the learning, not the pages of a national strategy. By repeating the learning loop cycle (prepare, review, do) you are far more inclusive with the class, as learning can be chunked up and reviewed as needed.

The final guiding principle behind the lazy lesson structure is to establish independent thinking and learning skills as part of your normal routines. Whilst most schools in the land mention 'independent learning' somewhere on their website, prospectus or school values poster, how many of these schools are actually doing it day in day out in the classroom is quite another matter.

Yet the lazy lesson structure lets you develop those thinking and learning skills in *every* lesson. The key: engage your students in a dialogue about learning. At each stage of the learning loop cycle, students review what they are doing and where it is taking them. After just a few weeks you will notice the impact of this on their learning and the growing ability of your students to articulate this clearly. Furthermore, when it comes to occasions such as academic mentoring, subject evenings, parents' evenings or whatever occasion your school uses to discuss learning, you will be able to have a conversation with your students that extends far beyond the traditional remit of how much of the new topic they understand. You might just touch upon the skills needed to be a learner.

And remember, you achieve all of this with three little words – prepare, do, review.

Now you understand the basic principles behind the lazy lesson structure, let's unpick each stage and give you some hints and tips for each one.

Phase 1: Prepare

The main purpose of the prepare phase is to create the conditions needed for the students to work on their own without lots of teacher intervention. As such, this phase covers the arrival and settling of the class and launching the task.

Learner–led starters

The purpose of any starter has to be to get the class ready for the lesson. That includes their emotional, physical and mental state. Sometimes it involves energising; sometimes settling (both of which, incidentally, can be achieved by playing the right music as students walk in). Lazy starters engage the students and give an opportunity for the teacher to make sure everyone is ready for learning. Examples of lazy starters can be found in Chapter 4.

Clear outcomes

Setting expectations for the learning and behaviour are crucial for both measuring progress towards a goal but also affirming high expectations with individuals. The Lazy Teacher may choose to have students setting their own outcomes for a lesson, especially if they relate to an extended learning project. For more on lazy outcomes see Chapter 2.

Lazy Task introduction

This is when the learning activity is introduced and the task is explained. Over time you can reduce the reliance on your own voice to do this and use other methods such as pre-recorded resources, your teaching assistants or other students.

Discussion questions for the prepare phase

Having a discussion about the process of learning is often as valuable as the thing they are learning itself. This is especially true when you are trying to train students into being more aware of their learning – what has been generically called 'learning to learn' in many schools. In light of the fact that, thanks to this book, you are beginning to teach differently, it is crucial that students are aware of the process they are going through as well as the content. To assist with this, you might like to call upon a series of questions

Meta Starters

What do you want to learn today?

What skills do you have that could
be useful this lesson?

What might hinder your thinking?

When have you had to think like this before?

What have you learnt that is similar?

What do you know that might be useful?

What are the signposts to your learning?
(must, should, could)

© Paul Bytheway, 2007

that can be displayed in the classroom to give all students an opportunity to reflect on their learning.

I have not seen a better way of doing this than the Meta Menu devised by Paul Bytheway, a series of metacognitive question prompts that get students thinking about the process of thinking and learning they are going through.

Used with a whole class, small group or even for individual reflection, these powerful questions offer tremendous support in your quest to push the responsibility of learning onto the students. They focus the students on the task ahead and give them time to think about how they are going to work (with the clever presupposition built in – you are going to work). Furthermore it enables cross-curricular links with other learning experiences, building upon student successes, which in turn helps self-esteem and motivation.

By building this discussion about 'How?' into your Lazy Lesson structure in the 'prepare' phase you are substantially improving your chances of students succeeding in the subsequent 'do' phase.

Phase 2: Do

Important note: the 'do' bit in this phase is them, not you! If the prepare phase has gone well you will now have your students working at full capacity and as independently as possible. It is the point when the Lazy Way is faced with its biggest and most fearsome opponent. No, not your head teacher but the over-enthusiastic teacher who cannot stop themself intervening, interfering and offering advice. The very same person, who, for fear of feeling redundant in their own lesson, has to be doing something with the students, regardless of whether they need it or not.

But please, just stop teaching! If you love them, let your students go!

If you have to do something, walk around the classroom gathering evidence of effective strategies being deployed by students to assist them in their learning, such as listening or taking turns to speak. You could feed this back via Post-it notes or even by means of a movie quickly produced on a Flip camera and shown at the end of the lesson.

Whatever you do, do not speak, as you will undo all the preparation that has gone into letting the students take control of their learning. To make sure you keep yourself busy and out of their hair, why not focus on setting up the following ideas to help students get on with their learning.

3B4ME

Or in non-text speak, 'What three strategies have you deployed before bothering me with your question, sonny Jim?' Insist on a culture that thrives on being stuck and finding a solution that is not simply to stop work, put up hand and wait to be spoon fed.

Brain, book, buddy, boss

This is a catchy way of getting students to remember the three other stages to go through before speaking to you. *Brain* refers to what they might know already but are just not thinking or making links. *Book* is simply what have they got with them – their own books or a friend's book, rough book, textbook or anything that might help them with some worked examples or a tricky key word. It could equally be 'board'. *Buddy* might be a friend or a nominated 'expert' in the class that has been charged with being the lesson support for this topic. It could equally well be the teaching assistant. *Boss* – they finally make it to you but if you do end up helping one of your students remember to ask for evidence of the Book, Brain, Buddy phases they went through before asking you. If you don't, the temptation to shortcut to you will be too great.

FAQs

Have a whiteboard where questions can be posted by the students. When someone posts a question only ever tell that person the answer and write the name of the person you have told under the question on the FAQs board. Anyone else in the class who wants to know the answer to that same question can talk to their class-mate rather than bother you.

Help desk

Set up a help desk with a variety of resources including help cards, expert students or computers to review any previous presentations or movie clips relevant to the learning, examples of students' work at different stages or even a 'phone link' to an expert or your teaching assistant. (I once saw this done in a KS3 RE lesson where students could e-mail a 'Professor of Philosophy' with their questions. In reality this was a willing sixth form student responding to their e-mails. Yet the awe and wonder was something to behold as these teenagers felt they were getting instant answers from a professor!)

Stuck–o–meter

Have a 'stuck' rating displayed in the classroom:

1 = not stuck at all   5 = bit sticky   10 = superglued!

Ask students to fill out a 'stuck-o-meter report' stating where they are on the scale and, importantly, what it is they need to know to get back on track again. In addition challenge them to find answers to the following questions:

1.   What bit of the task could you do if you moved on a step?

Meta Main Courses

What are you currently thinking about?

Has any of the lesson so far been about you?

What connections have you made?

How do you feel about the lesson?

How have you got involved in the lesson?

What should you do to further your thinking?

What breakthroughs have you made?

What do you want to know more about?

2. If I tell you this, what do you think you will be stuck on next?

3. Imagine you weren't stuck; what would you be doing? (OK, this is an outside chance, but sometimes tricks them into revealing the answer!)

The teacher I saw using this method explained that by making being stuck a real deep thinking moment, the students tended to avoid being stuck by working it out for themselves. Perfect by me.

Questions

Encourage students to use the Meta Menu questions without your guidance to try to unpick the problem. The Meta Menus are not displayed on the wall *just* to hide the damp patch.

Discussion questions for the do phase

You can use the Meta Main Course questions to really probe the thinking behind the learning. Unless the whole group will genuinely benefit, avoid stopping the entire class for discussion at this stage as it is more likely to be counterproductive and disrupt learning. Instead use this time to work with those students that would benefit from some additional support with developing the skills to make them better independent learners.

Phase 3: Review

Finally in our lesson structure we come to the review phase. As we know, this does not necessarily mean the end of the lesson; it simply means you have completed a 'learning loop' (which may mean the learning has gone well or conversely you may want to bring an individual, small group or even the whole class together to refocus on what should be happening).

Lazy plenary

The plenary is arguably one of the most potent weapons when it comes to recalling our learning. As it was once described to me: powerful plenaries make it permanent. There are two ways in which you might wish to deploy this weapon, with each deployment making your students better learners.

In the first instance you may be at the end of the learning loop having completed the stated outcome. Hence you will want to use the plenary to review the learning (content and skills) that has taken place. As we have already seen, this is not restricted to the end of the lesson. It is simply the end of a successful learning loop.

The other time that plenaries are deployed is when your students may be part way through a task and you want them to reflect. This might be because things are going well and you wish others to mirror the skills being shown by certain individuals or groups or because, quite frankly, it is all going wrong and your students need to start again by choosing a different approach.

Incidentally, I have observed many lessons which are wobbling around 'unsatisfactory' before being transformed by the expert deployment of a plenary. So whilst we have traditionally associated them with the end of the lesson, unleash this weapon at any time and watch the learning improve.

Discussion questions for the review phase

The review phase question consolidates the learning both in terms of the content – what was learned – and importantly, the process

Meta Desserts

How are you going to remember this learning?

What is the key aspect you will
remember from this lesson?

What has this lesson reminded you of?

Which senses were most important?

What did you learn that you didn't know before?

What have you learnt that could be useful elsewhere?

What have you learned elsewhere that is like this?

How will you apply what you have learnt?

© Paul Bytheway, 2007

– how it was learned. Whilst most likely to be the section that is axed due to time, it is arguably the most important. So make sure time is built in to allow this to happen.

Lazy end

This is all about marking the end of your lesson as opposed to a learning loop. And whilst you have got the students, you want to hook them into the next lesson. A sense of anticipation with a little ambiguous teaser about what is going to happen (such ambiguity not only enhances curiosity but also covers you if you are not totally sure what might happen next) is one of the laziest ways to get your students buzzing when they return next lesson.

The end of the lesson is also an opportunity to dismiss the class with some praise, encouragement and the odd enquiry as to how the netball team might fare tonight.

Incidentally if you want time to do all this, make sure your packing away routine is a lazy one and involves the students in putting away resources, picking up any debris from the floor and then standing behind their chairs. This bit is not just about being lazy, it is about respect.

Having been through the lazy lesson structure you could be forgiven for thinking that it seems like too much hard work and far from lazy. Just remember, though, that much of what is outlined above actually merges into the everyday workings of your classroom, with the students taking responsibility for many aspects of the three phases. In the experience of this Lazy Teacher, it is a very simple and effective structure which the students grasp quickly, enjoy and, in doing so, take those important first steps in understanding how to be a better learner. Before you know it they will be marching along the Holy Grail of Lazy Teachers everywhere –

the 'no-part lesson' where students proficient in the Lazy Way just get on and do.

So, give the Lazy Lesson structure a go. As an IT teacher once said to me, 'This will really defrag their learning.' Being an optimist, I have always assumed that this was a positive comment. If it wasn't, it was probably the worst someone could say about the Lazy Lesson structure whilst retaining an element of truth.

Chapter 4

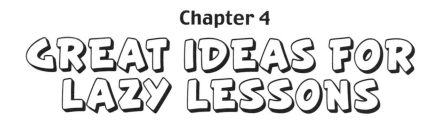

GREAT IDEAS FOR LAZY LESSONS

Chapter 4
Great Ideas for Lazy Lessons

Imagine the scene. It is your duty day and you have been tied up all through break with an incident involving a yoghurt and a pack of Pokémon cards. The bell went four minutes ago (and counting), and you know you have a Year 9 class waiting for you. When you finally get to your classroom, and a queue of restive-looking students, you remember that it is locked and the keys are in the staffroom. Returning a few minutes later, you are convinced that there are fewer students outside your room now than there were minutes before but you are too out of breath to care as you realise that your 'new term – new you' get fit pledge has not quite reached fruition. What's more, your lesson plan is in the car, through your classroom window you can see the computer is showing the blue screen of death despite being fine just twenty minutes ago and the head has just turned up to do the observation you had cavalierly agreed to yesterday. Add to this the fact that their exercise books are still on the kitchen table after your pre-observation marking frenzy last night and even your favourite students are beginning to turn on you and are staring and pointing at the sweat running down your face. Whilst 'crap' is not necessarily a judgement that the head would use, her looks do nothing to persuade you that she is not thinking it.

Surprised though I was to pass that particular observation and survive into my second term of teaching, I am not convinced that the events described above are the worst that could happen. No, far more soul-sapping are those occasions where you spend your entire weekend planning an all-singing, all-dancing, full complement of whistles and bells lesson that should last at least three weeks, only to have it sabotaged by the class who not only complete it in half a lesson (aided by Ricky falling off his chair and revealing where you had hidden the secret answer to question 5) but who also dismiss it as 'boring' and 'stupid' and why can't they just go on the internet or play hangman instead. And to think I could have been the regional manager for Currys.

I will confess that those were just two cringe-worthy examples from my NQT year (although the low point was a reprimand from the head for being a little too enthusiastic in a snowball fight with the students and making the self-appointed 'hard man' of Year 11 cry).

While you may not have been told off by a teacher for snowballing since you were 10, I would suggest that the first two scenarios – or something very like them – have happened to you at some point. If they haven't, don't feel left out, they soon will. And when they do, embrace them in a Lazy Way. Some of our best teaching and the students' best learning will happen when you have to think on your feet. There is an energy and enthusiasm that is generated by spontaneous lessons that you simply can't write into a lesson plan, and sometimes ripping up the intended lesson and going with your gut feeling produces something far better than what you planned anyway.

The trick when doing things the Lazy Way is to capture those techniques you pulled out of the bag in a crisis and employ them in a systematic, less frantic manner. However, don't think that being a Lazy Teacher excuses a lack of planning all of the time. Oxymoronic it may be, but 'planned spontaneity' is what we Lazy Teachers are looking for. After all, as Dwight D. Eisenhower once said, 'Plans are nothing; planning is everything.'

Great ideas for lazy lessons, then, is a box of tricks you always call upon to get you out of a tight spot in an instant. By their very nature, they put pressure on the students to fill the gap where your teaching was supposed to be and, in doing so, prevent you filling the void with some good old fashioned 'copy off the board' work or regaling them with tales of your trip to Goa in the eighties.

Given a little thought, any of the ideas that follow can be extended or reduced to fit into any part of the lesson. For example, a starter activity may work at several points when you start a new 'learning loop' (see Chapter 3 to learn more about learning loops). Or it may perform equally well as part of a plenary, of which there could be, or should be, several. What follows is a series of ideas that are unique in that you can arrive anywhere, anytime with anybody and deliver outstanding learning, primarily because you are making the students think.

To give you an idea of how long they might make your students think for I have classified them into three sections depending on how much time they take up in a lesson. (Although feel free to reduce or extend that amount as you see fit. It's down to you. Don't make me do all the work!) Or, expressed another way, they are categorised by how much time you have got left to persuade the head teacher observing you that you are not 'crap' after all.

Ten quick and lazy lesson ideas to have up your sleeve

Arrest me!

This activity really makes people think. It also works just as well with adults as it does with students. Tell the students that they have just been arrested and charged with being an outstanding learner/member of the tutor group/member of the school/historian/mathematician. What five bits of evidence would the prosecutor use to convict them? If there is not enough evidence, set them a challenge to accumulate enough evidence by the next 'court case' in four weeks time. You might just see a different response in how they work.

Choose a letter/number

Ask the student to choose a letter from the alphabet and a number between one and ten. Then, based on their responses, get them to come up with the specified number of words that relate to the subject you are studying that all begin with that letter. For example, it might mean they have to come up with seven words beginning with 'T' that relate to war poetry or one word beginning with 'Q' that relates to sustainability – either way it will make them think and have fun.

Animal memories

Ask students to choose an animal from a farm or a zoo. Then ask students to write any words associated with your chosen topic that begin with the letters of the animal. For example, if a student chose 'cat' and you were studying the Romans, they might say Centurion Amphitheatre Tiles. If the students try to spoil the game by just using 'dog' or 'rat' give them Parastratiosphecomyia stratiosphecomyioides* by way of punishment. It works every time.

Just a minute

Put students in pairs and give them a relevant topic. They have to see how long they can talk on that subject. Give your students some rehearsal time before showcasing different pairs in front of the whole class. Use non-performing students as an audience to pick up on any repetition, deviation or hesitation. As a slight twist, maybe it could be a minute of mime or drawing?

*You look it up.

Thunks®

Using part of the ethos behind Philosophy for Children, debate questions with no right or wrong answer. In his pioneering work in this area, Ian Gilbert coined the term 'Thunks' and in *The Little Book of Thunks* offers examples for use in lessons. If I borrow a million pounds am I a millionaire? Is it right to bully a bully? Is the hokey-cokey really what it's all about? Get students to create their own. It is a great thinking skill tool.

Killer questions

Get students into groups to create questions on a topic you have studied. These can then be asked to another group sitting on the 'hot spot'. Rotate the hot spot groups whenever they get a question wrong. Award points to make it a competition.

Frustrated by ...

Ask the students to create questions they want to know the answers to – the questions they are so frustrated by that they stay awake all night wondering what the answer is. For example, why is the sky blue? How is the bus timetable for the area worked out? When is your birthday if you are born on the first stroke of midnight?

What if ...

Rubbish bins gave you a £1 every time you put a piece of litter in them? What if door handles were made of chocolate? What if there were no such thing as time? Explore these and you might be surprised just what thinking and creativity skills you ignite.

Forrest Gump

Based on the Forrest Gump phrase, 'Life is like a box of chocolates' you can get students thinking without them even realising. Even better you can get them thinking without you being up all night preparing. Ask students to make a comparison between what they are learning about and another item, then sit back and watch them bamboozle you with some 'deep thinking':

The Second World War is like ... a garden fork because ...

Managing your finances is like ... a treadmill because ...

Quadratic equations are like ... a fish and chip shop because ...

I once heard a staff training session start with this activity using 'Learning is like a bag of salad because ...' My favourite answer from one session was 'because with the best will in the world, it wilts by the end of the day!'

Who would win?

If the following were to have a fight who would win: Basil Brush vs. David Beckham? A melon vs. an orange? A conical flask vs. a pipette? Winston Churchill vs. Barack Obama? Or in an animation themed tag team contest, Tom and Jerry vs. Wallace and Gromit?

Nine chunkier lazy lesson ideas to have up your sleeve

5–3–1

This is a way to generate many ideas and then focus in on one that you look at in more detail. For example, ask your students to write down five causes of the Second World War. Choose three that they think are the most important. For one of these, justify your answer. You can then extend this in many different ways. For example, get students walking around the room finding two people who disagreed with them.

Five degrees of separation

Link two items together in five steps. For example, if you were studying sustainability you might like to set your students the challenge of linking a tuna fish to their mobile phone in five steps. To give you an idea, here is one I've prepared earlier (although, in true Lazy Teacher style, I actually got a student to do it):

1. Tuna fish swim in the sea.

2. The biggest tuna fish contain chemicals such as mercury.

3. Humans eat tuna fish.

4. Mercury can be harmful to humans.

5. Humans use mobile phones which can contain mercury.

You may choose to use words connected to a topic you have studied or just choose some random ideas – either way students are thinking.

60 seconds to prove ...

You fully understand the theory of relativity, why industry locates where it does, the meaning of 'dulce et decorum est', how butterflies happen or where milk comes from. Whatever it is, your students have to prepare a presentation of exactly sixty seconds to prove they really do know it. This is a challenge about content as well as structuring a talk that fits a certain timescale.

Odd one out

Based on an old Paul Daniels game show (or is that old game show from Paul Daniels?) in which contestants had to determine the odd one out. Say, write down or show images from which students have to determine the odd one out. Set a challenge to prove why each one of them could be the odd one out.

Caption competition

Display an image from which speech or thought bubbles could be generated. You can source these from textbooks, newspapers or, if you are not too lazy to get your computer working, the internet. Get students to justify their comments.

What happened next?

Getting students to predict what might happen helps develop thinking and questioning skills. You could use a single image or a storyboard of images. The same principle works with a section of text from a speech or part of a story.

Create your own report

Based on self-assessment of progress so far, ask students to make comments about themselves as learners and what they are working to improve. Then ask the students to write their home address on an envelope (after all, they can do one envelope a lot quicker than you can do thirty). Keep them for a month or so and then send them home to the student with your comments. There is something curious about seeing a letter arrive with your own handwriting on the envelope, especially long after you have forgotten you wrote it.

Varied variables

Doff your cap to the work of the school numeracy coordinator and ask students to start plotting different variables on graphs. Do not be constrained by the norm though. How about creating a graph of time against happiness or plotting the emotions of a water molecule in its quest to fulfil every water molecule's ambition and reach the sea?

Blue Peter 'bring and buy' sale

Whenever you ask for ideas, in the first instance always ask for quantity over quality. To make sure you get real quantity ask students to stand behind their chairs (crucial, otherwise you will have people tripping over on the next bit) and then get them to mingle around the room 'bringing' and 'buying' ideas with the target of doubling the number of ideas they originally had. When they get back to their seats, it is time to select the *quality* ideas from their huge *quantity* of ideas.

Ten HUGE and lazy lesson ideas to have up your sleeve

How are you?

Spend time in a circle offering opportunities to talk about more emotive topics such as what is happening in students' lives, what challenges they are looking forward to or what dreams they might have. Switching tempo and showing a different side to you may mean you see a different side to them. With empathy and rapport crucial for an effective classroom this will not be time wasted. What's more, you won't have wasted your time planning it.

Would it be possible to ...

Give students a topic such as the digestive system and ask them what would be the most unbelievable way in which they could demonstrate their learning on this topic. Then ask them to come up with more reasons why it could happen than couldn't, covering all areas from finance to how props might be made. Before you know it, you have a group totally engaged in their learning and a whole load of other skills as well. It was how a group of students persuaded me to create a human mosaic on the school field and have the RAF film it for Comic Relief. Not only was their understanding of scale second to none (and far greater than had I waded through a series of different maps) but the footage was used on the opening sequence on the BBC1 *Comic Relief* show.

Judge and judgement

Set up a 'trial' and ask students to defend or prosecute characters. This is an activity that focuses on language, constructing arguments and etiquette, so start easy with scenarios such as Postman Pat is accused of drink-driving, before building up to cases such as defending someone who wants the right to chop down all the rainforests.

Police, camera, solution

Based on an idea I heard some years ago by Sue Cowley, author of many educational books, ask students to wait outside whilst you create a crime scene in the room. You could turn over a few tables, open a window, create a muddy footprint or two, dislodge a lamp fitting or ceiling tile, remove your keyboard and leave your lunchbox open with its half-finished contents on display. That should be enough to get their detective minds buzzing about what happened. If you are feeling less lazy you can order crime scene tape for about £15!

Rewrite history

What would have happened if ... ? Think of different scenarios that encourage students to consider how actions in the past shape what happens in the future. You might take on global issues, national issues or focus on something that has happened in your school. What would happen if the wheel had not been invented? What would happen if we had not discovered oil? What would happen if we lost the Second World War? What would happen if the school had won its recent unsuccessful bid for a new all-weather pitch?

Predict history

What might happen if ... England win the World Cup? they find a cure for all cancers? the Government bans cars? Extrapolate ideas based on different levels of extremism, for example 'very likely to happen', 'could happen' and 'unlikely but might happen'. This helps to train students in tailoring their responses to different scenarios.

I Resign

Announce your resignation to the class and say (and mean) that they have to teach the next five lessons on a particular topic. What is it they would want to learn and how would they do it, taking into account different approaches to learning? It is a great way to reinforce how they might learn effectively in their lessons and is ideal for spicing up revision lessons which more often than not see a reliance on teachers talking.

Media mayhem

Ask the students to present their prior learning or independently learned material in the format of a TV show. (Make sure the success criteria are based around the academic aspects of the topic, as they will naturally deliver on the more artistic side of things.) Whilst some might opt for a safe quiz format, be warned you might just see the Industrial Revolution covered in the style of the *Jeremy Kyle Show*.

Traditional and exciting

Lazy Teaching is not about ditching all the teaching strategies you have ever used. Rather, a few simple tweaks to one of your more traditional schemes of work can transform the 'ordinary but dull' into the 'outstanding but lazy'. For example, turn textbook learning into:

■ Timed or speed challenges when reading, making sure you vary the criteria and revisit answers at a slower pace for those who did not succeed first time.

■ Evidence hunt where students have to prove or disprove statements that you make.

■ Question, task, illustration or diagram ideas that would improve the textbook from the point of view of the learning. These could be sent to the publishing company, thereby cutting down on your marking and presenting the students with a real, and therefore engaging, challenge in one fell swoop.

And last but not least, the ultimate lazy lesson and the Holy Grail for all those who aspire to be lazy and outstanding:

Do nothing!

Tell the students you have nothing prepared but they have the lesson to do something that would help them be a better learner, subject specialist or even a better person. It could well be one of the most challenging things they have done. When they stumble, begin to unpick with the class what they could do. You should aim to have everyone helping everyone else to do something – from reading, spelling, listening, going through their fears and anxieties, talking about achievements, swapping homework ideas, writing a letter to a friend, mapping out a revision plan or whatever else they feel they need.

All these ideas can be adapted to any age or any subject and all have one thing in common – they can lead to outstanding lessons with no preparation, no pointless marking and assessment (thus eliminating the biggest time consuming factors in teaching) and they are great fun for you to deliver. Even better, what you will soon realise is that you have a growing repertoire of great ideas that you can reuse and recycle time and time again. All of which means that the next time your lesson plan is in the car and your computer is on the blink, it might be you are about to have your best lesson observation yet.

Chapter 5

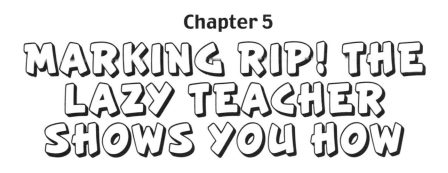

MARKING RIP! THE LAZY TEACHER SHOWS YOU HOW

Chapter 5
Marking RIP! The Lazy Teacher Shows You How

There's one thing worse than spending your entire Sunday afternoon marking books. It's spending your entire Sunday afternoon trying to relax, knowing there are books to mark but you just can't bring yourself to do it. But you know they are there. Waiting for you. In that plastic box. In the boot of your car. Unmarked. Waiting.

And how you wish you had opted for that bottom set group at the beginning of term. Every lesson with them might end up a Prozac-inducing circus but at least if they do write it's on the tables and not in their exercise books and the marking of homework is never an issue thanks to an unspoken agreement between you and them – 'You don't spoil my weekends, Sir, and I won't spoil yours.'

No, you had to get that top set where every piece of homework is ten sides of A4 in pursuit of that Snickers bar you offered for the best essay. And to make it worse you just know they have the sorts of parents who will be going through their children's books in search of red pen and favourable comments.

Yes, we're talking about marking. The teacher's curse. The worst part of the job. The Bermuda Triangle of the long, relaxing Sunday afternoon.

I've been conducting my own informal research on marking recently, especially the matter of teachers and homework. During the course of this investigation I have discovered that there are two great places in which to conduct research - staffrooms and wedding receptions, both of which are environments where you'll find teachers seated together, the latter being a vaguely curious phenomenon. You can almost hear the bride's mother saying, 'She's a teacher as well, so they're bound to get on' and overlooking the fact that you may just be sitting a 'flog 'em and hang 'em' type next to a 'hug a hoody' *Guardian* reader, or someone on the table has just suffered a bruising Ofsted, leading to an unfortunate incident with the Eggs Benedict when asked the question, 'Oh really? How did it go?'

As informal as my research often is, it does suggest that I am not alone in my reservations about marking. Nor am I alone in having suffered that car park phenomenon that is 'marking envy' – the overwhelming feeling of jealousy that hits you when talking to a colleague in the car park whilst simultaneously trying to work out why they are not carrying three Aldi carrier bags of marking home with them like you are.

Or, to put it another way, marking is quite simply the most laborious part of what is actually quite a good job. For this reason, I vowed that my Lazy Way was going to extend to marking and assessment. Why should marking succeed in driving me out of a profession I love? Surely that is what the students are for?

The first thing to establish is the difference between marking and assessment. Without wanting to start an unnecessary debate and stir up too much academic rancour, I find it important to distinguish between the two, as it will help you to grasp the Lazy Way when it comes to assessment.

Assessment is any form of feedback – verbal, written (including e-mailed) text – from myself or other students.

Marking is feedback that includes a justification of a grade of some description.

Now, your criteria for marking and assessing may be linked to some nationally agreed standard or equally may be a set of criteria designed by the class. It doesn't matter. Likewise, it doesn't matter whether the grade comes from me or the students because I train the students to be as good at marking as I am. And so should you. It makes for more relaxing Sundays.

But what becomes of that precious Sunday time that you actually have spent on their work? How annoying is it, after all the effort that goes into marking and assessing, when the students skim read your well thought out and neatly written comments before diving straight for the grade or mark out of ten? After a brief consultation with their mates as to who has done really well or who has had a howler, you then witness the page being turned and off the class go in search of another 'learning' experience.

And, even if they do read it, how do you know if your efforts and time spent on marking and assessing are having an impact? Assessment and marking must surely be a two-way activity. With the amount of time spent on marking and assessment every week, it is vital that everyone feels like they benefit from the process and that it is able to help everyone become a better learner or, something that is often overlooked, a better teacher.

What's more, there is also one other great reason to explore the benefits of the Lazy Way when it comes to assessment and marking, namely praising students. Praise is something that is often in short supply in education and not just for the students. So a marking and assessment ethos should surely correct that. And that doesn't simply have to be through the medium of the student's exercise book.

Regardless of whether the subject you are teaching has exercise books or not (and if it does, are you really sure you need them?) the Lazy Teacher's approach to marking and assessment is adaptable to all forms of work. Carried out effectively your approach to marking and assessing could be *the* significant driver to improve standards in learning. What a Lazy Teacher should never do, however, is mark purely to satisfy a marking policy which, in turn, has been written to satisfy a misplaced parental need for ink on the page, not thoughts in the brain. The difference between the two approaches could well be the difference between having a long Sunday lunch in the pub, or not.

The key thing to remember is that how you approach lazy marking and assessment is actually heavily reliant on how you approach lazy lesson planning, so you should be looking to pre-empt that boot-full of books by giving greater thought to the tasks that the students are going to complete and how they are going to be assessed. Key questions you should ask yourself to plan the assessing and marking elements of learning are to be found in the following section but, before you even start the process, there are two key questions to ask that permeate the entire Lazy Way:

What role will I have to play in this?

What role will the students have in this?

Or, put more simply:

What's the least amount I *have* to do and what's the most they *get* to do?

It never ceases to amaze me that many teachers do not make the connection between teaching and learning and the quantity of books they have got to mark of an evening. If your lesson goes something like, 'Turn to page 64. Read up to page 68. Answer questions on page 69 and 70 if you have finished. Thank you everyone. I need to take your books in for marking,' then you will surely pay the price for such ill-considered lesson plans and deserve never to see *Rugby Special* all the way through.

A lesson such as this will typically generate thirty books containing text-dominated answers, with the odd appearance of a diary based activity for those reaching the extension task. If you agree that the option of *not* doing anything with this work leads to resentment from the students and accusations of being unprofessional from colleagues and parents, then you have just created a whole lot of work for yourself. And there's only one person to blame. To add pedagogical irony to the misery of losing your Sunday, with a lesson like that there's probably not a great deal of *actual* learning to mark, assess and build on anyway.

So, have a look at what the Lazy Teacher is suggesting. The ideas are subdivided into different sections that enable you to emulate the Lazy Way in planning, delivering and feeding back after the learning activity. The bits of marking that are left after you have implemented these ideas (and there will be and should be some) will be purposeful, effective and will not take you long. You never know, you may even be the cause of the car park envy at your school.

RIP marking – getting the planning right

1. Ask yourself key questions

Never set a task without asking yourself the following critical questions:

What will be produced?

How will it be presented?

How can it be assessed?

Who will assess it?

What role will I have to play in this?

What role will the students have in this?

By spending a little more time thinking about the outputs, you will influence what you give as the inputs. Furthermore, my experience has shown me that you will improve the process as well.

2. Plan your focus

Have a focus for your marking and assessment that can be communicated to the students. It goes without saying that people have a greater chance of succeeding if they know what it is they are being measured against. Likewise, ask the students to identify something for you to focus on, such as where they have improved their spelling, presentation or explanation of points. It is very disheartening from their point of view if you do not pick up on their progress.

3. Do it differently – do it the Lazy Way

Choose to do things differently. Whilst some of the ideas take time to set up, you will save time in the long run as you will be able to repeat the formula with different classes. These ideas are an entirely red pen-free zone – which might just be why they go down so well with the students.

■ Could student work be assessed through a voting system at lunchtime, for example, as an art gallery or poetry performance on the stage? If you have the technology, you could use electronic voting pads. If not, use paper voting cards that can be dropped into a ballot box.

■ Use school events such as parents' evenings, careers conventions, school plays or academic mentoring days to show off what work the students have been completing and invite feedback and comments. Similarly, could you create an exhibition of work at a library assessed by the general public? Each piece of work could be rotated to the 'Comments on this one please' position on the display board to make sure there is coverage. Student displays should be a demonstration of students' work remember, not your ability to mark it.

■ Could you have a 'guest marker' such as your link governor, the mayor or the local history group? These people often thrive in getting involved with educational projects (and feeling important).

■ You could post YouTube movies on the internet and use comments taken from this global population (with a subsequent lesson on e-etiquette probably a must!). This gives a chance for students, parents and colleagues to share in what you have been doing.

■ You can create a whole range of different assessment criteria if, for example, you film a group's presentation then play it back to allow more considered evaluations on score cards. It has always amazed me how challenging this is for groups to do, yet they always enjoy doing it. Furthermore, you do not even have to say anything, but the next time you film them, the students certainly do not make the same mistakes again. This has been some of the best assessment for learning I have ever done.

■ You could extend the lazy way into your colleagues' classes by getting your class to present to a colleague's class and use their feedback for marking and assessment. In the spirit of collaboration though, it would seem only fair that the other class presented something back. And don't worry if the classes are different ages. In my experience you'll find it helps.

■ Get students to keep learning journals (not necessarily written) so the process as well as the product can be assessed. It makes a refreshing change to look at work that is neither right nor wrong. It is what they did and how they felt that provides the useful reflection. Similarly get students to use learning journals to capture what you or other students have said about pieces of work. Students can review these comments as a starting point for future bits of work.

■ Use these ideas not as a one-off special occasion, but as part of your learning routines. If you can get your students to relish the assessment it makes them very keen to do the task well. Motivation and marking all sorted – the Lazy Way.

4. Plan to use students

Students can learn a lot by completing the marking. Simply swap books and mark. If the success criteria are clear it is a tremendously powerful process for all ages. You can even get the marking checked and verified or complaints settled by having an appeal system with students articulating why they feel they have been marked too harshly or, heaven forbid, too generously.

Alternatively, display work as a 'gallery' and equip everyone with Post-its and ask them to leave comments on five different pieces of work. Make sure you are clear about what the students are commenting on – ideally it is the very things you shared with the students in your success criteria. Students love coming back to see what has been written by so many different people.

5. **Plan for no assessment and no marking**

    Dare you? Does every single lesson need to be monitored? I am not advocating anything less than outstanding throughout this book. Having periods of time with no marking and assessment still fulfils that.

RIP marking – what to do before accepting work in for marking

1. **Communicate the focus**

    At the launch or during the start of the learning experience communicate the assessment focus. Why would you not do this, having planned your assessment focus? Get the students to plan how they will know that they are working towards achieving the focus and allow time for them to check their work *as they go along* – otherwise it is a bit like giving the builder the plans for your new extension when he has finished building.

2. **Give students checking time in class**

    Give students five to ten minutes in class before they hand in their work to check it thoroughly. Value this time and develop strategies to give students ideas of how to check. For example, they could swap books and ask a partner to check or look at some exemplars that you have available. The key is that they engage in this checking phase. With many students finding this bit boring, you could follow the lead of one teacher I saw who had introduced a fine system for any mistakes which were meant to have been corrected, such as capital letters for names of people. The twist here was the fine was given not to the person whose work it was but the person who was checking the book! Peer assessment has never been taken so seriously.

3. **Check from the end**

   Tell students to check their work starting from the end. They read the last sentence, then the second last sentence, and so on. This helps them to focus on the details of each sentence such as grammar or spelling rather than the overall sense, so there should only be one stage in the checking of work.

4. **Do me out of a job!**

   Ask students to write the comment they think you should write and justify why by writing comments in the margins of really good pieces of work that meet the success criteria.

5. **Encourage experimentation and risk taking**

   Encourage students to experiment with new words and expressions by including them in their written work and indicating that they are experimenting by putting a question mark and a comment. Explain that you will get credit for these – not penalties.

RIP marking – giving the work back

1. **Review time in class**

   Give time in class for students to read through their returned work and to ask you for clarification. Make sure they correct any remaining errors and make a note of them *there and then*.

2. **Mark corrections**

Ask for students to go through their work again, make improvements and have them peer assessed. This way, you will make sure that at least two people have actually looked at your comments – the person who has made the corrections and the person who is going to have to mark them.

3.   Stop history repeating itself

Ask students to start the next piece of work by recording somewhere (as it may not be in an exercise book) what area they will be working on with this piece of work based on feedback from previous work. It might be to spell 'occasion' correctly, to have used a greater range of colours or to have spent more time listening. It doesn't really matter what it is. It is the process and awareness of learning that is important.

4.   Focus on good points

Occasionally, do not correct your students' work for mistakes, but rather *only* focus on the good points. It is natural to avoid comments that give us loads of extra work or give us a negative impression of our efforts. (Just imagine if your performance management review had taken such an approach – how might have you felt and behaved during the next year?)

5.   The late night marker

This was an idea which stemmed from complete exhaustion and trying to fulfil a promise that the group would have their fully marked books back next lesson. In short, I wrote a load of incomprehensible rubbish and got everyone's names wrong in their book. The student response shocked me. They were so quick to say why the comments were not applicable and what I should have written instead that they were basically demonstrating to me what wonderful markers they could be. So why not return their work with some completely fictitious comments and ask them why the comment or final grades are wrong?

6. **Mark the marking**

Ask students to mark your feedback in terms of how it helps them learn. There is no point in wasting time on something that does not work. Do they like symbols, targets, you taking a whole page to write your comments in a style that is an illegible crossover between a doctor's prescription (pre-printed ones of course) and Egyptian hieroglyphics.

RIP marking – assessing group presentations

Assessing class presentations can be challenging. Firstly, you have to break down the perception that the students can bring to such lessons: 'Nothing is going on today is it, Sir? We're just watching those presentations!'

Secondly, you have to ensure that the assessment is genuine, accurate and engages the whole class. Whenever you let the vast majority of the class become inactive the situation can easily become stressful and lead to conflict and behaviour issues. So, the obvious answer is to engage them. In doing so, student learning extends beyond the task and into the presentation stage as well. Why would just a teacher be marking and assessing the work when the watching audience will have valid views and constructive comments that they too could contribute? Additionally, how can the teacher alone assess and mark fairly if they are constantly scanning the room for students staring out of the window, playing cards or simply trying to make the presenter laugh? The Lazy Way demands that all students are involved. And having tried many different methods, here is the way that works, every time.

Simple steps to get your students assessing group presentations effectively

1. Set success criteria and allocate marks to each of the criteria. This then becomes the basis of your scoring grid that every student will need for each group presenting.

2. All groups assess each presentation using the agreed and explained success criteria allocating marks after each performance on their scoring grid.

3. In order to improve the assessing skills, you allocate each person a group that will offer both summative (the scores) and formative (the justification in words) feedback. And this is why the method works, as they take peer feedback very seriously.

4. Students then give their mark sheet to a group member to whom they offered summative and formative feedback, meaning no one keeps the mark sheet they were scoring on as it has gone to the person you were writing about. This mark sheet is stuck in the book/file/portfolio of the person being assessed not the assessor's. This helps to raise the quality of the comments.

Marking and assessment carried out the Lazy Way transforms a part of the job that is often dreaded into something that is quite exciting and is integral to the learning experience.

What's more, if you are not already buzzing with excitement about how you can slash through your marking for the rest of term, I still need to share my favourite part of the Lazy Way …

The 'feel good Friday' phone call

The feel good Friday phone call is something I try to do every Friday and it works like this.

Choose three students whose parents/carers you are going to ring to say just how well their children are doing. Be specific to start with – for example, you may be ringing about a particular piece of work – but then expand your positive feedback to cover their more general characteristics. Never lie, but make as much as possible of their achievements. From the initial sigh and fear at the other end of the line, the assumption being that something has gone wrong, comes a deluge of uplifting comments about how they must be enjoying your lessons, thanks for all the work you are doing and look forward to hearing from you soon. It means that everyone, if you have planned your lessons properly, goes into the weekend feeling great and loving being part of the school.

Isn't that so much better than a dose of car park envy?

Chapter 6

IT - THE LAZY TEACHER'S FRIEND

Chapter 6
IT – The Lazy Teacher's Friend

Let's get one thing straight. Under no circumstances does the Lazy Teacher attempt to keep abreast of new technologies. It is an impossible task with 'outlandish' becoming 'new' and 'new' becoming 'mainstream' in the blink of an eye, and something that was cool and trendy that you could drop into a conversation with young people to prove how 'with it' you were can, overnight, end up revealing just how pitifully ignorant you are about the whole technology thing. (Try telling your Year 10s you are looking to set up a MySpace account or, sin of sins, talking about 'blogs' and not 'tweets'!) Keeping up with technology trends is, quite frankly, not that appealing to the vast majority of people and anyone over the age of 20 who does so is the sort of person you don't normally see when the sun is out.

The use of technology in the classroom is a gift for the Lazy Teacher, as not only can it cut down on work, but you are invariably surrounded by IT experts in your class who will work the technology for you. On a visit to a school recently I was offered help with my new mobile phone by the 'Technology Help Desk'. It was a service offered by students for the whole school community for a nominal fee that was a fraction of what you would pay someone from the 'real world'. The students told me that staff were by far the most frequent consumers, adding learning and enterprise skills plus enhanced self-esteem to the experience of the students involved, not to mention a sense of superiority.

It is the role of the Lazy Teacher to harness the principles of what IT can do, turning your classroom into one big 'docking station' for all the wonderful stuff that is out there. Yet just because it is

IT doesn't mean you have to abandon the Lazy Way. Far from it. Can you enhance the whole student learning experience by sitting back and getting them to take the technological lead? Oh yes!

This chapter explores six principles of the using IT the Lazy Way. These principles are then backed with numerous practical examples showing how you can integrate them into your lessons. I have even offered a little more detail to the examples, as my conversations with teachers suggest that, despite great emphasis on IT training, there is still a lack of confidence in using technology in lessons. This isn't helped by the fact that there is still a tendency in schools to have an 'IT lesson', assuming that is, against all odds, that you managed to book the 'IT suite'. (The whole idea of having an IT suite is to me like having all your eggs in one basket, locking it, putting up a basket rota and then expecting everyone to make great omelettes.)

Remember that all of the ideas suggested make for perfect homework opportunities as well – whether that's completing the task or creating new resources to be demonstrated next lesson (and for you to claim as your own and use for evermore). In my experience, students will certainly make very sure technology works if it means they are the ones showing it off. Or alternatively, follow the idea of a colleague who has computer 'monitors' in each class (and by this I mean children in charge of IT, not a load of screens). Not only have the monitors lowered his stress level, but the post is highly sought after and never abused, despite the obvious temptation and ease with which students could do just that.

Funny what happens when you do less yet demand more.

Lazy ideas for achieving Principles 1 and 2

Principle 1: Technology should be used to switch on learners. Having the technology at your fingertips means the mood can be easily and effectively set for any lesson. So hit them with the full audio-visual experience the minute they walk through the door!

Principle 2: Technology should be used to keep learners engaged. Once you have grabbed them keep them grabbed for as long as you need to by using technology for introductions, big pictures and overviews of the lesson, modelling the process and the outcomes and creating interactive presentations. But remember, big, bold and brassy will work, but not forever. So, get the students to join you in launching and presenting what the class is learning by asking them in advance to lead and launch the lesson. Show how the process will unfold with animations and clips of effective thinking about problems to be posed.

Sound waves make brain waves says Nina Jackson

Use music to get them in the right mood for learning. To energise your students play music with 125–175 beats per minute. Tracks like 'Simply the Best' by Tina Turner, 'Wake Me Up Before You Go-Go' by Wham!, 'You Spin Me Round' by Dead or Alive (or maybe even something from their own decade!). To calm them down, use music with 60–110 beats per minute such as 'Paint the Sky with Stars' by Enya or 'CinemOcean' by Anastasi. (For many more ideas about how to use music and what music to use take a look at *The Little Book of Music for the Classroom* by Independent Thinking Associate and music for learning guru Nina Jackson.)

What are they saying?

Project images of well-known or interesting people, add a speech bubble and ask students to come up with – and justify – what that person might be saying. This is a very simple yet highly effective way of delving into feelings and emotions. For example, a picture of a grieving family next to a hospital bedside could offer a way in to talking about pain, suffering and voluntary euthanasia.

Volunteer please!

Create a random student selector with the student stopping the selection process via a PC. This can be achieved using basic functions on PowerPoint (honest!). Once you have the software you could use it to select words randomly to revise, topics to learn, in fact, just about any aspect of your lesson.

Watch it!

Have a movie clip playing on a loop via the projector so when students arrive they can instantly start work on the open question that you have set relating to the clip. Once everyone has arrived and is working, ask for answers to your question, getting the student to pause the clip on the part that best helped them in coming up with their answer. It is important to have an open question to enable your students to be occupied for as long as it takes for everyone to arrive and settle.

Clocks and timers

Use the board to display giant clocks and timers for tasks to inject real urgency and genuine (not teacher-controlled) time. These are freely available on the web. Just type 'free stopwatch' into Google – or get a student to do it …

Camera, lights, action! I

Take pictures of the lesson and then use free web based software to make a dynamic slideshow set to music. This simple process will help them to recall what it is they were doing and help bridge the gap between the last session and your lesson now, without you having to lead an embarrassing starter consisting of you saying, 'And who can remember what were we doing last lesson?' followed by complete silence.

Camera, lights, action! II

If you are studying a certain geographical location then get a web-cam link from there to show what is happening right there, right now, giving your classroom a real window on the world. You can pause the feed on certain images that could provide discussion points. Really interesting ones for the Amazon, for example, can be found through simple Google searches.

The headlines

Run the lesson with BBC or Sky News on as your projected 'screen saver'. You might be surprised what subliminal learning takes place. In doing so you are mirroring the resource rich environment that your students are used to. It goes without saying that you might want to preview what is being displayed but it can be very exciting to suddenly incorporate sudden breaking news into your lesson.

The next train will leave ...

Use technology to make audio and visual announcements that can be played on a timer. You could quite easily build up a bank of jingles and announcements meaning you will never ask a group to pack up again!

And now it's time for the adverts

Advertisers rely on us looking at different images over time to build up an opinion about a product. Could we do the same with learning? When you are not using the projector, you could try to show key messages or resources related to the topic you are currently studying. You could flash up deadline dates, extra sources of information or even clues if you are carrying out an investigation. I have found it a fascinating and highly effective way of getting messages across.

Hit or miss?

If a student or group has worked well in the lesson offer them the opportunity to play some of their music whilst you are packing up or have it as the music everyone hears when they arrive next lesson. You can even have a bit more fun by asking the class to decide if the music is a hit or a miss!

Lazy ideas for achieving Principles 3 and 4

Principle 3: Technology should be used to review what has been learned. One of the most valuable aspects of technology is that it can assist us in reviewing and recalling prior learning, the very thing which we know to be crucial to embedding our learning so that it becomes permanent. Technology should therefore be used to record the learning process as well as the learning content. After all, no Lazy Teacher would want to waste time drawing the same diagram for those five Year 8 classes you happen to teach.

Principle 4: Technology should be used to empower learners. Like the proverbial hot potato, get the technology out of your hands and into the far more capable and willing hands of the learners as often and for as long as possible. Interactive technology is just that – a shared resource. That brand new interactive whiteboard in your classroom is not just a special toy for you, so get over it and make sure they are using it more often than you are each lesson. By getting IT into the hands of the students you are enhancing their learning and providing them with the skills they will need to further that learning, both in and beyond school.

Going live in 4, 3, 2, 1 …

When you are using group work (following the Lazy Way of doing it, of course) make sure one group works on a PC projected onto the whiteboard rather than pen and paper so the whole class can see the process that group is going through. It is a powerful and wholly appropriate message that you value content and process.

Blockbuster!

If a movie clip needs to be played again, or paused by a group or individual, give them opportunities to do so on another playback machine. This means the whole class does not have to watch it again and you are encouraging students to take responsibility for their learning.

What were we thinking?

Let groups capture their thoughts and ideas with a variety of IT resources such as Flip cameras, mobile phones and Dictaphones, assuming the business studies department (formerly secretarial skills course) still has some. Playing back a discussion not only refreshes your ideas but also enables the group to analyse their group work skills.

Be lazy!

Create movie clips designed to assist students in the drawing of difficult diagrams. You might even want to send them to their mobile phones so the students can pause the clip whilst they get the drawing just right. Then when they are ready they can press play again for the next phase – a modern, IT-rich version of painting by numbers. (Oh, and if their mobile phones are banned or in their bags, what message is that sending them about being creative with our learning processes?)

Help me out here!

Give students on-line access to resources, models, advice from other students, animations, previous work success criteria, previous FAQs – in fact all they may need to succeed. You can build up these resources every time you teach the topic and, just like the websites they may well visit, ask students to score the most useful resources in your help section.

Stuck for music?

Ask students to bring in their iPod or other MP3 player or even, wait for it, their mobile phone with music tracks on it. Then they will have – or will get hold of – the track they want. They are your biggest resource and student self-esteem soars when they feel they have contributed to the lesson.

Student teachers

No, not that tall, nervous looking chap who used to work in a bank, but the class in front of you. You have a whole class of people who, sorry to break this to you, may well deliver the lesson better than you. Let them design lessons and then deliver them, insisting that they use all the IT equipment. You will instantly generate resources as well as tap into the contagious nature of peer-to-peer learning as they battle it out to see who is in charge or who can deliver the best lesson. You never know, you might learn something along the way as well.

Journal thoughts and feelings

Ask individuals to record thoughts and feelings about their learning in your lessons or in mentoring sessions. Set up a delayed e-mail so they can compare how they feel now with how they would feel at a point in the future. It is important that students connect with the usefulness of IT over and above word processing, as they may well be entering a world where even word processing is defunct.

Lazy ideas for achieving Principles 5 and 6

Principle 5: Technology should be used to link the learning process together. Technology these days is increasingly designed to work with other technologies, linking people and experiences like never before. Bring in as many different technologies as you can, from iPods and Flip cameras to Xboxes to mobile phones, and use your classroom as the docking station to end all docking stations. Everyday technology can add to the learning process and help motivate students to engage with your lesson away from the confines of your allocated slot on the timetable. And remember you aren't just linking the technology – video conferencing, webcams, blogs and tweets all link people like never before.

Principle 6: Technology should be used to link learners together. So much of our educational culture is built on the 'one-strike' learning model which demands that students 'get it' there and then, or miss out, lose out and fall behind. This is soul destroying, demotivating and an entirely unnatural way of learning. The use of collaborative learning spaces to share ideas, thoughts and feelings is a great way to overcome this.

Games for learning

Whilst *we* might not spend hours on our Xbox or Nintendo DS Lite console, many of our students *do*. Try to harness their skills with this equipment by challenging them to play some of the educational material that can run on them. Students could bring in the hardware and you provide the software – after all, it is a modern day version of the 'bring in games on the last day of term' scenario we all know and love from primary school.

AQA – any questions answered!

Text a question to 63336 (it only costs a pound) and they will respond with a 'well researched and educated answer'. Can your class beat the phone? It sets a tremendous challenge which, with a careful bit of manipulation e.g. putting your phone on silent in case the answer comes through quickly, can have the class working for the whole lesson like never before.

Caught you being good

Use your projector to display 'assessment for learning' evidence in the classroom. This might be pictures, live movie footage or typed comments. Alternatively you could run a live scoreboard during a task using a simple Excel spreadsheet – a very lazy way to add lots of excitement and tension.

Lesson design – on the cheap

There are hundreds and thousands of on-line resources from little gadgets and gizmos to full blown presentations. Use chatrooms associated with exam boards or just use Google to find resources

for your interactive whiteboard. Every search will reveal some-thing.

Class war!

Give students inter-group challenges by using interactive websites that permit multi-player use or where there is a leader board. Some websites are designed for groups from around the world to play each other but are just as effective when you are pitched against a team from just down the corridor. Many can be used from home or on mobiles and as such offer great opportunities for homework. If you are not sure what an educational interactive website that offers a multi-player game is - just ask the students to provide you with some. If they want to play they will find them.

Blogs and chatrooms

Post a picture and get everyone in the class to pose five questions about it. Then vote for the five best ones the class would most like to explore. This really gives ownership of learning and allows for collaborative thinking in a safe, password-protected environment. It could also be conducted off-line in the classroom.

Flip–ping brilliant!

Use Flip cameras to capture the learning and then play it back to students who could then analyse what was effective. Groups or individuals could collate views and opinions and bring them back to the whole class to share on the 'big screen'. This is a great way to review learning progress (and hair styles) over any period of time.

Is Skype hype?

Make phone calls and conduct video conferencing around the world for next to nothing. Through organisations like Global Leap you can get yourself linked up with other businesses, educational organisations and schools to swap information and find out information on the topic you are studying (for example, one colleague did a live link to a dive on the Great Barrier Reef).

Considering I am no geek when it comes to the use of IT in the classroom, I was surprised how many ideas I have used over the years – and remember this is by no means an exhaustive list. Then it struck me just how many had been the result of the students leading the learning and coming up with great techniques and ideas. Even better, many of their ideas focused on recording the process of learning, not just the end result.

So, not only have I integrated IT into the students' learning following the principle of the Lazy Way (as essentially they did it) but also they have developed strategies to help themselves become better learners. There are not many national strategies that can claim that.

Our learners are changing. Technology is very natural to our students, the 'digital natives' as they have been called. For future generations it will be even more so. My 5-year-old son Henry quite happily navigates his way through his favourite websites using a mouse or can make amendments to documents I am creating (you may come across some in this book). My 3-year-old son Oscar already jabs at the screen in an attempt to activate the parts of it he wants. In light of the new touch screen technologies he'll be proficient with an iPhone before I am.

Across all our schools there are classrooms of students who already engage with a whole gamut of ever-changing new technologies, which means half our job is done. Great news for the Lazy Teacher. The best things we can do for these students is to ensure we do our part of the job properly, namely keeping up to date with the pedagogy of using IT. But in the Lazy Way, of course.

Chapter 7

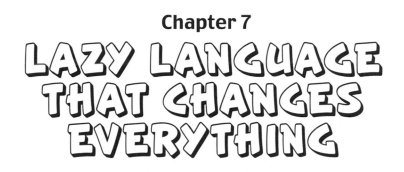

LAZY LANGUAGE THAT CHANGES EVERYTHING

Lazy Language that Changes Everything

The name is Bond ... James Bond.

James Bond

Go ahead, make my day.

Dirty Harry

Frankly, my dear, I don't give a damn.

Gone with the Wind

Please be quiet now. Oh, come on everyone please. Err ... you are wasting your time not mine. Now, that really is enough. I am aware the bell has gone. The bell is for me not you. We can wait all night – I have plenty of marking to do ...

Scenes in a Classroom

OK, so the last one is made up. But if you did have a famous phrase in your classroom, what would it be? If it is anything like what my students told me during my first years of teaching, 'Shhhhhh', 'OK guys' or 'Errr right then' may possibly feature highly on your list. The Lazy Teacher avoids such phrases, instead substituting them for a script that has a positive impact on students' self-esteem, motivation and behaviour.

Not only that, the Lazy Teacher also considers both *what* we are saying and *how much* we are saying. Too often, excessive verbal communication limits any opportunity for learning, with all the time taken up by the allegedly instructional teacher-talk. So, whilst you offer a full and detailed explanation, the class are drifting further off into blissful sleep or starting to engage in low-level disruption. Be honest, you know what I mean! (And if you're still not sure, think about staff meetings you have been to and the frustrations you have felt as the presenter repeats themselves over and over again, before pronouncing those fatal words: 'Any questions?')

Minimising the amount of time you spend talking is the simplest thing you can do as a Lazy Teacher to give your students every chance to genuinely learn in your lessons. Fearful of talking too much in sixth form lessons I devised a game that not only meant I couldn't waffle on for too long without being stopped but also had the students hanging on my every utterance. I simply set myself a maximum limit of words that I could use in the lesson. By giving myself, say, 200, I really had to think about the impact of what I was saying. The same effect can be had by setting a time limit for how long you can talk to the whole class. The students, warming to this idea, even started counting my words or timing how long I was speaking for. Without realising it, they were now inadvertently listening more closely to me than they had ever done before. If I ran out of time or words, I was often amazed that the students could carry on from where I finished and go on to complete the work. Lazy teaching and independent learners, all from one little game.

You can also have some outstanding learning happening without any verbal communication from you at all. There are now some simple animation software packages (for example Crazy Talk) where you can animate images to talk to your class – leaving you to just smile and point at the screen! Ever fancied having Sir Alan Sugar deliver an enterprise challenge or an animated figure give out instructions, call the class together for a recap or even ask students to tidy up and wish them well as they leave school? Well now you can. The worrying thing is, they often respond better to this than to the teacher. Is this a true testament to the Lazy Way or a simply a worrying indictment of the twenty-first century? You decide. Either way, it works.

Lazy language that changes everything, then, focuses on lazy communication in three crucial areas: self-esteem, motivation and behaviour management. And we know all of these are inter-linked and have a direct impact on learning. However, I have separated them for the purposes of this chapter, as I wanted to highlight their individual importance as well as their collective impact on group rapport – arguably *the* crucial element in achieving excellence in the classroom.

What follows is a selection of practical ideas that will give you the basis of your Lazy Teacher script. However, avoid the trap of post-training keenness that sees you attempt all new strategies in your very next lesson. Even great phrases need limiting.

Phrases that enhance students' self-esteem the Lazy Way

Over the course of their education, your students will be grappling with physical, emotional, social and economic aspects of their life that will all have a bearing on self-esteem. Yet whilst self-esteem is part of a complex jigsaw and is not something that can be simply sorted or pinned down to one particular area, we know that it plays a part in determining behaviour, academic success and indeed enjoyment of the whole school experience. The use of the following phrases to improve self-esteem, therefore, needs to be done in a genuine, continuous and on your part, heartfelt manner, with the body language to match. Ever convinced someone you are having a good time when your face is saying something else? So, don't expect your students to be convinced either.

Remove the threat of failure and heighten the sense of challenge before a task begins

'I know this is hard yet we have made so much progress. I wonder if we could ...'

'No other group has managed this, but I think you might be the group to do this.'

'I bet you can't ...'

Promote previous successful learning experiences

'You really seemed to enjoy it when ... Let's use that approach again.'

'Think about the skills we used when you were successful in doing ...'

'Last time you were stuck you were able to ...'

Take blame away from them and role–model learning yourself

'I'm sorry, I did not explain that very well ...'

'Who could help me explain that better?'

Avoid general and give specific, interesting, instant and varied praise

Avoid: 'You have all done very well today' and replace with, 'I like the way you ...' or 'I feel really pleased when ...' The use of 'I' is harder for the students to discount and you are demonstrating a personal attachment to the events in the classroom.

Pitch your feedback to the individual. At times be minimalistic and start off with private praise before going public. Teachers can crush a student's image and turn off learners in a matter of seconds!

Show progress over time: 'Last week you achieved ... and this week you have achieved ...' or 'You have got so much evidence to show how you have progressed. What piece are you most proud of?'

Activities to promote students' self–esteem the Lazy Way

Hero for the day

Ask students to draw, act or write a fairy tale in which they are the hero or heroine.

Selling yourself

Ask students to make a commercial about themselves. You might need to try this as a group task for those with low self-esteem.

My favourite thing is ...

Get students to discuss, write or draw their favourite activity, toy or hobby. I have used this with students of all ages. It is only the content that changes, not the passionate work they produce.

Coat of arms

Ask the students to design a coat of arms that includes pictures and words that reflect what they're good at and what values they have.

Display boards

Have pupils' work exhibited in the classroom on big display boards. If you get the students involved in the planning and creation of the display, not only will their self-esteem soar (and not just the person promoted to being in charge of the staple gun) but also you will have a ready-made security force to protect the work. Change the displays regularly to make sure everyone gets their work displayed.

Make us happy

Ask students to draw, act or write about a special 'happy place'. Discuss what steps you could all take to make your learning space more like the place they are describing. As you will have guessed, it is really an opportunity to steer the conversation towards rights, responsibilities and values rather than working out how you could install a BMX park. Although as I write that ...

Feel proud

Feeling proud is an emotion that you should always be allowed to display. No one has the right to take away one of the most amazing emotions we feel as humans. Make a bulletin board titled 'I am proud of ...' where people can display pictures, work achievements and life events (e.g. birth of a new family member).

WANTED!

Create 'Wanted' posters that display all the good qualities of each individual.

Phrases to improve motivation the Lazy Way

Motivation is a very personal thing. But it can be influenced. If I think back to various times at the schools I attended, I can cite examples of when teachers were incredibly motivating. So, and stand by for the gooey moment, it is true – teachers can change lives. Yet conversely I also recall how much fun and liberating it sometimes was when a teacher was absent and we were left to our own devices. In fact, the whole Lazy Way ethos partly stems from these two educational memories or, as I once waxed lyrical on the back of my train ticket after a particularly heavy meeting in Manchester:

Inspire and motivate when you speak,

But never dominate and leave them weak.

The students need to be motivated, yes. But motivated to work independently. If they are only motivated when you are in the room, then something is wrong. Not only that, there is a limited employment market for those needing permanent supervision and guidance. The sooner we – and our students – realise this the better.

Use loyalty, respect and an innate desire to be better than their peers to motivate

When you find yourself struggling to motivate and inspire individuals you are in danger of slipping into bad habits and abandoning the Lazy Way. Try to use your students' loyalty and respect for their peers to nudge them towards being an engaged learner. They might feel comfortable letting you down, but can they face up to their mates? Using that logic, these phrases may just get your students behaving in the way you want:

'Your friends are relying on you to become experts in your area in order that you can complete the task.'

'The work is being assessed by other groups and not by me – so think how you are going to beat the other groups.'

'Your team mates need the skills you can offer to complete this challenge.'

Make it RING

Pre-exposure and big picture techniques prepare students for future learning and take away the fear that students can feel when unsure of what might happen: 'In today's/next lesson/next we are going to be ...'

As Independent Thinking associate Dave Keeling states in his book *Rocket Up Your Class*, you should always link learning to something that is Relevant, Interesting, Naughty and a Giggle. That is to say you should make it RING! With that in mind, it was full marks to the business studies teacher who I observed linking political elections and fiscal policy to the costs of petrol, and in the process had his sixth form class of aspiring and newly qualified drivers on the edge of their seats: 'Have you ever wondered how the government's views on the economy could mean you pay more for your petrol next year? And might you be interested how you can avoid paying that extra money by exercising your right to vote?'

And if you worry that your new subtle lazy ways will be lost on your students, let them make it RING for themselves with this approach: 'Give yourself a reason why this might be useful for you now or in the future. Now swap reasons with five other people in the class.'

Remind them of their goals

'Remember why we are working with quiet voices.'

'How will we feel when we achieve our goals?'

'What target did you set for this piece of work? What are you doing to make sure you achieve the target?' (You will find that this one does not warrant an answer from the student as they instantly modify behaviour and revert to being on-task.)

'I know it is fun to catch up on gossip/your e-mails, however, now is the time to concentrate on our work.'

Give opportunities to achieve goals

'So we can be one step nearer achieving our goal: you have two minutes to mark your work/the person's next to you and then ten minutes to amend any corrections.'

'Can you choose the order in which you want to work, as only you know how you can best achieve the goals we have set.'

'Tell me three things you are really proud of with your work.'

'Put a star by the three things that you do not want me to miss and show you have achieved your target.'

'What is it that you have enjoyed most about this work?'

Activities to improve motivation – the Lazy Way

Map progress in a visual way

If you provide a facility to track the learning that is taking place in a visual way, for example, a graffiti wall where students can write all over a display board covered in lining wallpaper (it is by far the cheapest way of doing it) you can clearly demonstrate that learning is taking place. And when they realise that, perhaps your Lazy Way is something they will buy into after all.

Give them choice

Let students choose the genre in which they produce work – movie, radio show, artwork, poetry or sentences. If they achieve the outcome and students use a balance of mediums over time it does not matter which approach they take. Make sure you praise risk taking when a student chooses a different format of work and even generate scenarios when this happens by having a random format selector, such as a spinning wheel.

Competition

Set up the process of learning as a competition. Group work, for example, is a perfect opportunity for your students to lay down the gauntlet to another group and declare that they will beat them! Nothing will get in the way of a victory over old rivals.

'We have started so we will finish'

When planning your lessons, build in time for the completion of work rather than just insisting that students catch up at home or allowing tasks to drift off because you have run out of time and the scheme of learning has decreed that you have a computer room booked in three weeks' time and you must complete certain activities before your one IT lesson for the year makes any sense. A sense of completion is important and will influence how students feel about their learning (and, by default, your lessons).

Phrases for managing behaviour the Lazy Way

Managing behaviour in the classroom is often revealed to be the most challenging and complex aspect of being a teacher. Be it your first ever class, or simply a new class, it would be most unusual not to wonder how they will behave and, just as importantly, how quickly their behaviours could change.

Behaviour management is an ongoing game, with no winners and losers. To have winners and losers is to seek a control method based on fear and hierarchy which in turns leads to resentment and further poor behaviour. Recognising that behaviour management is a game (and I find it removes the personal stress if you do), the Lazy Teacher looks for strategies that avoid certain flashpoints and puts the right corrective strategy in place at the right time. Remember that the game will have started before the students arrive in your classroom as they, like you, will have been influenced by events outside your classroom. The previous lesson, an incident in the playground or en route to your classroom or trouble at home will all bear an influence.

The vast majority of behavioural issues in the classroom are high frequency and low severity. But over excitable or ill thought out strategies can soon change this. An incident over Robert and Ricky sharing a pencil can very quickly become a much more involved incident if you let the primary behaviour (not sharing) be overtaken with secondary behaviours (refusal to cooperate, rudeness, furniture kicking, etc.).

This is where the Lazy Teacher focuses and avoids the admirable magic trick of creating a mountain out of a molehill as it is at complete odds with the Lazy Way ethos. Firing off ever increasing sanctions for the primary behaviour (not sharing some resources) and then for the secondary behaviours (the conflict) means you soon run out of options and have nowhere to go.

As with self-esteem and motivation, I have put together a script. To help even further, I have given you 'Robert–Ricky' phrases that you should *not* use (although I appreciate this is not necessarily the best idea, as simply telling someone not to do something is actually misinterpreted by our brain. How many times have you touched the plate after a waiter has told you, 'The plate is very hot, do not touch it'?). Use the phrases as an alternative to the long winded, public floggings that are stressful and achieve little. Simple phrases can be very effective. Just ask Bond. James Bond.

Lazy and far from outstanding phrases and actions that do not help manage behaviour

These are not included as a tempting opportunity to play with the behaviours of your students. They are included in case you recognise yourself using them in your current script. If you do, as a matter of urgency unlearn the phrases now, especially if you are using them in conjunction with non-verbal communication, such as pointing, invading space and a raised voice.

■ *'I didn't hear that, what did you say, Luke?'* – you probably heard first time; do you want to hear it again? If you do, revert to a written statement or a quiet conversation away from the heat of the moment.

■ *'James, pull yourself together boy'* – personal and unnecessarily derogatory.

■ *'David, I didn't think you were as childish as this'* – again, personal and unnecessarily derogatory.

■ *'Why did you do that, Bruce?'* – often an impossible question to answer and if they do, the answer normally is thrown back in your face, for example, 'Because Theresa did'.

■ *'Sally, this is the worst example I have ever seen'* **or** *'You are always late, Tom'* – avoid potential factual discussions!

■ *'You are much worse than your sister, Anna'* – sibling rivalry rarely works in this context.

Now that we have dealt with those let's move on with the ideas that will let you be lazy and outstanding with behaviour management.

Lazy and outstanding phrases and actions that do help with behaviour

These phrases are especially effective when combined with nonverbal communication, such as open handed gestures, plenty of space between you and the pupil and spoken with a calm voice. If you can adopt an almost surprised and disappointed facial expression as well, you will be well down the route of perfecting the Lazy Way of improving behaviour.

■ Blame the behaviour not the person – *'Wendy, this behaviour is not like you. I am surprised to see you doing it'* or *'Your behaviour today is not what you have done before, Sam.'*

■ Give a misbehaving pupil space and time and get them to give their account using an opening line of *'Jack, what's the issue here and what can we do to change it?'*

■ A simple refocus and clarification of the task with the student is a non-threatening, non-judgemental approach which will get you the behaviour you want without conflict – *'Britney, I'd like you to get on with your work, thank you'*

■ If there is an unavoidable delay before dealing with an incident use – *'Nina, I can see you are upset and I will be able to help you in two minutes.'*

■ Try reversing roles with the student – *'Henry, if you were me what would you do to resolve the situation?'*

■ Self-deprecating humour can sometimes diffuse a situation (but never at the expense of students) – *'Can you imagine how I felt when I fell off my skateboard whilst trying to impress the girl I'd fancied for ages? I was embarrassed, much like you are now.'*

■ *'Maybe and ...'* – when several groups are talking you need to start somewhere! When confronted with *'But others are doing it, Miss'* use *'Maybe they are and now I am speaking with you, Amy.'*

■ Acknowledge pupil feelings – *'Matthew, I can see why you are upset, however ...'*, *'I know why it happened Ashley, however ...'*

■ Offer choices – *'Okay 8B, would you like to complete this task now or after school?'*

■ Self-correcting behaviour – *'Oscar. (Pause) What are you doing? (If they respond let them finish) What should you be doing?'* This works really well for low level chatting especially if combined with a slow walk towards the student to whom you are talking.

■ Use *'It'* messages – *'It makes me feel frustrated when students walk around the room because it stops us from learning.'*

■ Acknowledge part of the problem, however small – *'I can see it might be irritating to be told to do something that is boring Cheryl, however this is what we have to do today.'*

■ Use name (pause) instruction (pause) and thank you – *'Grant (pause) sit on your chair properly (pause) thank you'* and walk away, giving a non-verbal assumption this will happen (use the eyes in the back of your head to make sure it does!).

The phrases in this chapter (apart from the ones quite clearly identified as being of no help at all) will help the Lazy Teacher build rapport, as they are correcting those annoying high frequency, low level disruptions that form the vast majority of classroom disturbances. They are aimed at correcting those sulky learners that cannot be bothered and want to chat. I will leave you to see if they work on your colleagues ...

Chapter 8

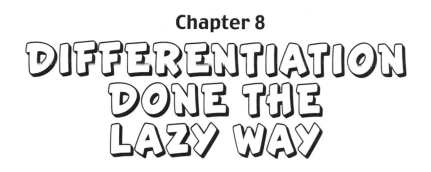

Chapter 8
Differentiation Done the Lazy Way

As you have probably come to expect by now, the Lazy Way means that you should not worry about differentiation as something else to do. Outstanding teaching is all about differentiation. Which means this whole book is about differentiation and shouldn't really merit its own chapter.

Or so it would seem.

I have always been intrigued by differentiation, not least as it was portrayed during my teaching training as a 'controlled substance', dispensed by those with qualified teacher status to those identified as being in need. Yet despite the d-word being bandied about on PGCE courses, in the Training and Development Agency professional standards and by Ofsted, very rarely will anyone talk about how to actually differentiate. And when they do so, it seems to involve thirty lesson plans for thirty people — which obviously is not the reason you picked up this book.

It therefore makes sense to include a chapter on it so, at the very least, we can build a bridge between knowing we should be doing it and wanting to know how to do it. Then it will be your turn to take the lead and say to anyone who cares to observe your new lazy ways, 'I had just the right amount of differentiation in that lesson.'

So let's put this controlled substance under the Lazy Way microscope and reveal the rules of lazy differentiation.

The three golden rules of Lazy Differentiation

1. Differentiate for all-through variety (and that's a variety of approaches spread across the term, not all in one lesson).

2. Ask other professionals in your school, the class and, where appropriate, individuals what differentiation they feel is needed.

3. Make differentiated strategies clear to the class so they can learn to differentiate for themselves. It is vital to remember that differentiation should not lead to dependency.

And whilst rules may seem a little strict and prescriptive, it is perhaps worth thinking about what benefits these rules offer to you and your students:

■ You will design engaging and highly effective lessons.

■ You will reduce time spent on creating inappropriate differentiated resources (as well as the humiliation of having them skidded back across the table at you).

■ You will be overtly promoting the process of learning, which all too often is kept the guarded secret of those in possession of a teaching qualification (and we know that these people alone cannot drive up standards, otherwise it would have happened by now).

It is this last benefit, looking at differentiation as something to be shared *overtly and regularly*, that is crucial to the Lazy Way. Undertaken as part of your 'normal lesson', it will soon outperform any dedicated learning to learn package the school may have in place. Just like learning a new language, it is far better to be immersed in it all the time rather than study how to learn in period three on a Thursday. If the students are having the process shared with them all the time, they will soon start to follow the process themselves.

Differentiation does not come any lazier than a student who recognises the need to sit in a different part of the room to help them with their learning. Or the student who knows they can re-watch the short movie you have just shown on the school intranet and play it back, pausing when needed. Perhaps your lazy differentiation will mean your students will automatically use the unmanned 'help desk' that has extra ideas and tips on it or use the nominated peer 'lead learners' for the lesson.

And where does that involve you? Well, if you have followed the Lazy Way and made students aware of the learning process, you never have to accept the defeatist, 'I am stuck' as a reason for a student being off-task. Because then you simply ask them, 'So, what have you done to help yourself?' (see page 55 3B4ME)

Differentiation done the Lazy Way categorises ideas for differentiated activities that genuinely enable you to help students help themselves. This is where the true Lazy Teacher should concentrate their efforts. Thinking in advance how you might differentiate frees up time and space during the lesson to concentrate on aspects of the lesson that really do need your support, rather than running around helping despondent learners, their raised hands wilting as fast as their motivation for your lesson, who quite clearly do not know what to do.

This list is not definitive because, as I have been at pains to point out, differentiation is really just effective teaching, something which does not condense into a neat list.

The strategies primarily focus on ideas that will support what we may call the 'less able' students, yet could be easily skewed to support whatever group you choose – reinforcing the view that differentiation is for all.

Lazy Ways to differentiate your learning environment

Displays

Have a variety of exhibits including student work that change regularly. Use pupils to design and put up the displays.

Plants

Have plants on display that are looked after by the students. Tomato plants are cheap (and could be bought with a class collection or donation) and provide a fascinating learning tool as well as a sense of belonging. Remember to give the plants names. In my experience, it helps to keep them alive!

Get outside

Use the spaces outside the classroom. Some students will learn better outside. Ever heard someone standing in the rain justifying their job by saying, 'Doesn't matter about the weather, I could never work inside'? I wonder how they felt about school?

Seating plan

Have a seating plan to provide consistency as well as a variety of seating options from single desks to group desks to provide choice.

Whilst furniture should be moved around, it is reassuring to have a base.

Sit on ...

Vary the style of seating in your room from time to time. Some people will work better on the floor, some a bean bag, some a chair. It is unlikely that thirty identical chairs will be matched by thirty identically shaped students. Sometimes take away the furniture or use it to let the students build structures in the lesson. From medieval castles, to chambers of the heart to parts of a production line, the humble table and chair might just help the penny drop for some of your students.

Are you a hot or a cold thing?

Your room will invariably have warmer and cooler parts to it. If not create some and make these obvious to the students. Some will thrive on a bit of warmth, others including your tomato plant will wilt. You will notice a tremendous change in approach and attitude when you get this right.

I wonder

Improve curiosity and intrigue by collecting weird and wonderful items to put on your desk or shelf. Awe and wonder can engage the most reluctant learners. I have seen a bendable Elvis, dancing flowers and even a duck that chooses volunteers all seamlessly used to get students thinking. Remember to change your props regularly, as familiarity breeds contempt, even with ducks. The laziest way to do this is to ask students to look out for things they could bring in.

Rights and responsibilities

Always have written, pictorial and verbal expectations of how the environment is going to be respected through a mutually agreed charter.

Lazy Ways to differentiate the task

You do it

Give the students both the confidence and encouragement to design the task for you. Sounds simple enough, but how many times does it happen? If you tell them that they need to set a challenging task – they will pitch it just right. If there is some key learning or a skill you think you need to cover, make this explicit in your brief to the class so the students can build it into their work. They cannot guess what is in your head.

Blooms

Vary the progression, number and style of questions that you use in the classroom. Use Bloom's Taxonomy to ensure appropriate challenge for all. You could even have a differentiated copy of the taxonomy on the wall so students can begin to expect the questions you might be asking. If they know what is coming they can start to prepare and take away some of the fear of learning.

Too much text

Think carefully about what actually needs to be written onto a resource or worksheet. Too much text poses an unnecessary challenge for some learners. You might just be better off explaining it (and recording your explanation so it can be played back whenever the learner needs reminding).

Start simple – finish clever I

In your lessons progress from concrete to abstract – in other words have a low access point leading to a high challenge. For example, in a maths lesson you might start by asking, 'What is half of four?' but finish with 'What is half of love?' Delivered the other way round and you will have chaos and confusion.

Start simple – finish clever II

Use simple, open stimulus questions to generate a discussion rather than wading in with the heavy hitters. For example, 'What do you do on a Friday?' whilst seemingly dull can explode into lots of different areas when the student gives you a response to work with. You could quite easily be having a discussion about culture, religion, family or jobs with your students in seconds. The difference is that this way round you have given them a non-threatening way in using language and a concept they can understand.

The high jump

This is another idea that came from a student who could not understand why, in maths, he had to do ten examples of a sum when after a couple it was quite clear he could do it. He suggested allowing students to use the 'high jump' approach – that is to say they can start the challenge just before you think it is going to get too difficult for them. I totally agree. There is no point in students completing work (that needs marking or assessing) that has proved nothing, other than the fact that it is too easy or too hard.

Not me!

Make it clear where they can seek help other than from you. Without that direction is it no surprise the hands shoot up straight away?

For this you have ...

Two minutes, ten minutes, an hour, thirty seconds. If you vary the time allowed for a task you will vary the nature of the learning that goes on. You might want rapid fire quantity over quality or you might want creative deep thinking. Either way set an appropriate time limit to foster a sense of urgency. Just when they get used to the amounts of time you tend to give certain tasks, change it all around. A debate about who is going to be jettisoned from a hot air balloon is suddenly done in sixty seconds and ten types of vegetable (that no one else will name) can take sixty minutes!

Matching learners

Think about how groups can be constructed, as different combinations will spark off each other differently (and for lots of reasons). For one task pitch friends against each other and then use them next time to cooperate. The same old people, in the same old team, around the same old table will give you the same old results. Just look at your senior leadership team.

How would you help yourself?

Ask students, in an appropriate way, what it is that is needed to help them learn better. You might not get an instant response as, to be fair, who will ever have sat them down and explained what could be on offer? A Lazy Teacher would because just like they cannot guess what is in your head, you cannot guess what is in their head either.

Lazy Ways to differentiate the launch of your learning

The review panel

Ask selected students to preview forthcoming tasks and make amendments to your resources and lesson plan that they think would make it clearer for the class. When they have fed back, surprise them and truly follow the Lazy Way by telling them that as they understand it fully, they can now launch the lesson!

Variety is the spice of life learning

Offer a variety of ways in which students can produce work for you. Does it have to be written or the dreaded poster again? If you are unsure of the format of the suggestions the students make ask them how and by whom the work can be assessed and marked.

Modelling

If appropriate, or indeed possible, model how the task might look at different stages – be it content or process. This might be something that you can build up for the next time students are learning about the topic but more often than not you will have a pioneer group that is always a little bit ahead.

Camera, lights, action

Think what could be recorded in audio or visual form in order that students could have access to the instructions at a later point in the lesson. It will save you repeating yourself and means students can access help as and when they want it without bothering you.

Know your data

Just for clarity's sake, I do not mean just the Scholastic Assessment Test, Cognitive Ability Test, Fisher Family Trust or teacher-assessed levels. I mean passions, ambitions, dreams and inspirations (and if they haven't got this then help them to generate it). Use all the information about your learners' prior achievements and backgrounds to build a picture of your class. If you have three-quarters of the rugby team and half the hockey team in your class you might, on occasions, want to give your learning a sporty contextual setting. Could they study speed, time and distance by looking at the location of rugby grounds or the venues for the Olympics?

It may be you have a class which loves performing, or animals, or food. Build this into your planning and their learning. If learners can believe it, they can learn it. Using real places, real people and real passions creates scenarios that will stimulate students' interests, meaning they can be motivated to push their own boundaries. Result – one of the hardest jobs is done for you. How lovely and lazy is that?

Having thought about your room, the task design and how you will launch the task (if indeed it is you who will launch it) there is one final piece of the differentiation jigsaw – high expectations for every single member of that class. By ignoring student reputations and demanding high expectations you are achieving two more goals without any preparation whatsoever.

Firstly, you are being refreshingly different in not perpetuating the label that a student or a class may carry. After all, how many people does it take to tell us we are a little overweight before we become very self-conscious? Behaviour is not far behind. Continually telling someone they are poorly behaved will lead to poor behaviour. Fortunately the opposite can be used to great effect. Contagious, meaningful and relentless (but justified) praise can be equally as powerful.

Secondly, you are being dismissive of some of the barriers that will have appeared in their lives. Albeit hard to pin down where they come from, barriers pop up that prevent students from thinking they can do something. Boys excelling at ballet? Girls studying engineering or manufacturing? Of course they all can. And they do. The common theme that such rare success stories have is that the young people have been encouraged by someone who has set high expectations and will not buy into the idea of limiting barriers.

Differentiation is not about running around the classroom with different worksheets typed in a variety of different fonts with the odd word missing. It is so much more – much of which requires no effort from you. Share the different strategies you are using with the students themselves, be explicit about the process of learning and insist on feedback about which strategies are working.

After all, why would you want to waste Sundays developing differentiated lesson plans and resources that are not going to benefit your students?

Chapter 9
THE LAZY SEAL

Chapter 9
The Lazy SEAL

Question: How many educational initiatives have the same name as an animal?

Answer: One, SEAL (Every Chinchilla Matters doesn't count and Building Schools for the Fuchsia is about flowers).

So was it genius or luck that this strategy, dealing with emotions, empathy, intelligence and love, spelt the name of a mammal that happened to be one of the cutest, cuddliest creatures that waddles this earth with a ball on its nose?

The Social and Emotional Aspects of Learning (SEAL) strategy recognises that not only can you be intelligent in many different ways, but also you *should* be intelligent in different ways. Using emotional intelligence is crucial to surviving in the twenty-first century (it probably was in previous centuries as well – we were too busy killing each other to notice). The professions now recognise that, when you bring together what neuroscientists, psychologists, educationalists and yes, let's face it, children, have been saying for many years, a greater emphasis must be afforded to these critical elements in the learning mix.

So, with the right sort of image in our minds (unless you're a Canadian hunter) it's important to realise that SEAL is not a great deal extra on top of what good teachers do anyway and, as such, is ideal for the Lazy Teacher to exploit to the full.

With so many educational policies it is hard to remember all of them so here's a quick rundown so we all know what we are talking about. Common across all key stages, there are five strands to SEAL as follows:

1. Self-awareness

2. Managing feelings

3. Motivation

4. Empathy

5. Social skills.

Why these strands? According to the Department of Children, Families and Schools they underlie almost every aspect of our lives, enable us to be effective learners, get on with other people and therefore be responsible citizens who presumably will have something to contribute to society.

I agree. While take up of the strategy is patchy depending on individual schools and teachers – and let's face it there are many other bandwagons for schools to jump on – this is a particularly good one for improving learning and can be implemented wonderfully using the Lazy Way. So, if you feel the school is not hitching itself to this particular wagon well enough, have a go yourself. You will be surprised how many colleagues join you.

In the Lazy SEAL I will take you through my favourite strategies that help you embed SEAL in your lessons and across the school. They are not precisely aligned to the various strands of the SEAL strategy, as often more than one of the strands is covered by each activity, and they are primarily based on your choice of language and how you set expectations in your classroom. Because of that, there is no preparation, no fuss and nor do you have to rely on having the right bit of technology. The ideas are simply based on a desire to have better learners in the classroom.

Lazy Ways for incorporating SEAL

When planning lessons simply build in opportunities for SEAL to happen. Take something straightforward like decision making to begin with and encourage it from individuals, groups and the class as a whole. Learning to live with decisions and understanding their consequences is very important. Likewise in a group or class context, accepting choices that may not have been your own is equally essential. So, build in decisions for the group about how they will present their work. Maybe someone would rather write an iPhone application as opposed to producing a poster. And if you feel happier with a traditional pile of posters to mark rather than an iPhone application, remember the Lazy Way mantra – you are planning lessons for them to learn, not for you to teach.

In the first lesson (and then ongoing)

Class rules

When agreeing class rules and expectations which support respectful behaviour (e.g. 'no put downs'), make sure the justification of the rule is included as well.

Relationships

Build warm relationships with the class: meet and greet, use names, use quality listening, offer frequent reassurance and encouragement, and so on. If you do not like them, pretend you do. It might just work.

Praise

Recognise and celebrate effort, perseverance, resilience, empathic responses, good social skills and positive behaviour, and say why such behaviour is good for learning *and* life – because not everything is just for the classroom.

High five!

Give at least five positive statements to every negative one aimed at correction. This is quite hard to do, but you'll be amazed at how quickly the classroom culture will change. A simple strategy is to praise those who are doing what you want, not to bemoan those who aren't. It's what Ian Gilbert calls 'catching them in, not catching them out'. For students seeking your attention, they will soon realise they get it by doing what you ask.

Peer praise

Encourage peer-praise and self-praise based on skills and content. Think how we like it when a colleague praises our work – students are no different. Yet it is not always that easy to say 'well done', so create formal and informal opportunities for this to happen. I was once told that praise counts for even more when you say it to a third party in the hearing of the person you are seeking to praise. Give it a go (and not just in your classroom).

Stick to the rules

Intervene immediately when there is inappropriate behaviour and don't ever let things build up. Treat emotional misbehaviour as you would any other type of misbehaviour. In doing so give precise and clear feedback about what was inappropriate in their actions and remember, it is the behaviour that is wrong, not the student.

Feel the behaviour

In discussion about behavioural issues or any incidents, talk about the feelings associated with what has happened. Use a restorative approach and, for those of you new to this, see if you can spot the difference between the following two columns:

What happened?	What the hell is going on here then?
What were you thinking at the time?	Why on earth did you do that?
Who has been affected by what's happened?	OK, I want names ...
How were they and you affected?	You can stay behind afterwards and think about the consequences of your actions.
What can be done to make things better for all concerned?	Right, detention and a letter home for you, my boy.
What can be learnt so that something like this doesn't happen in the future?	People like you never learn ...

Each new lesson is a new beginning! Be prepared to start afresh after making your point and listening to their point.

Remain aware that some students who lack social awareness will need support and a bit of scaffolding when working in groups. They may, for example, find it difficult to negotiate with others in their group. To overcome this simply allocate roles within the group, something that the students will eventually do for themselves. You can make it clear that you need someone to chair a discussion or insist that comments have to be written down or that the team nominates a time keeper so no individual can hog the discussion.

And despite what Arnie might say, this time it's *not* personal. It very rarely is, so don't take their behaviour to heart. By the time the bell goes and both you and that naughty Year 10 boy are lighting your first cigarette on the way home from school, he will have forgotten what just happened. So, try to remain calm in the event of behaviour which you can feel is stirring up negative feelings and thoughts in you. Remember, everybody acts in a way that serves them and maybe their attention seeking behaviour, much as it needs to be corrected properly, is a reflection of the lack of time and care and, yes, love, any adult has shown them in the past.

After lessons and around school

Wherever you lay your hat ... your rules apply

Recognise behaviours that you have been working on in your classroom and whenever you see them being duplicated around the school, say so. If someone is cooperating and queuing nicely for school lunch, say so! If someone is looking neater than they usually do, tell them! If someone stops running down the corridor the minute you come around the corner, praise them for walking!

Be interested

Always enquire about the sport results, how the school play is going or any achievements out of the classroom, so you link the skills and attributes that students will have used to become county netball champions into their learning. Similarly, mirror the skills they used to learn their lines in the school play when helping them to remember the formula for photosynthesis. By making them realise that they already have the skills for learning you are seriously weakening their 'I can't do this' excuse.

How was that?

Invite feedback from students to say how learning has changed in your classroom. Ask them to choose one thing that has improved. They might not articulate the change in the words of the SEAL strategy, but you will soon see what can be traced back.

Having SEAL based outcomes

The following list provides some SEAL related student outcomes for you to build into your overall lesson plan. The SEAL outcome could be additional to other learning outcomes or integrated within an overall learning outcome. Always use outcomes within the Lazy Lesson structure by making them explicit and revisiting and celebrating progress made. For SEAL based outcomes, you can promote discussion by asking: 'What would I see if this outcome is being achieved?' or 'What would I hear if this outcome is being achieved?'

Some of the listed outcomes are similar in nature but have a slightly different emphasis. Choose those that are most appropriate for your group. Feel free to adapt them by, for example, breaking them down and making them more specific or adding new ideas and creating bespoke outcomes. The list is not exhaustive – I am far too lazy for that. After all, the students are more than capable of generating them and often set far more of a challenge than I would have done.

SEAL outcomes

■ Contribute effectively to group work

■ Communicate and express my ideas effectively

■ Listen effectively to what others say

■ Break a long term plan into small achievable steps

■ Set myself a goal or challenge

■ Give and receive positive feedback and constructive comments

■ Compromise when there is disagreement

■ Take into account another person's perspective even if I don't agree with them

■ Resist distractions

■ Persist with a task even when it is tricky

■ Concentrate for increasing periods of time

■ Utilise strategies that help me concentrate

■ Identify my strengths and feel positive about them.

Like many of the ideas within education (new or otherwise) they can often be dismissed with a flick of the hand and either an 'I am already doing that' comment or a dismissive 'I have already done that' statement. Yet, as Dr Andrew Curran says, to learn we need the heart to be happy before the brain will engage (and if you are still sceptical, forget the neuroscience and just think of your own experience in the classroom as a child).

The need to have happy hearts as a stepping stone to fully engaged brains will never be more important than for the generation we are currently teaching, where the continual explosion in knowledge in the twenty-first century needs to be matched by a similar explosion in our ability to learn. These are learners who are in a newly competitive, globalised, 'flat world' and are subject to more social pressures than perhaps any previous generation. SEAL is your way to really equip young people with what they need to succeed in that environment. So, don't let its cute and cuddly name deceive you. It's a jungle out there ...

Chapter 10

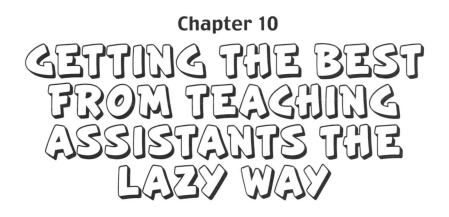

GETTING THE BEST FROM TEACHING ASSISTANTS THE LAZY WAY

Getting the Best from Teaching Assistants the Lazy Way

Can you honestly say you know the name of every teaching assistant in your school? If you teach in a primary then perhaps you do (and I bet that's not just because of the smaller number of adults in the staffroom). Overall the number of teachers who can complete this challenge is too low. Yet the lazy use of teaching assistants, or indeed any competent adult who strays into your learning environment, is crucial in making learning both highly effective and fun.

And knowing their name is an important starting point.

Teaching assistants play a crucial role in supporting the work of the teacher and ensuring that all pupils make progress in their lessons (something which you may have noticed Ofsted have decreed to be a characteristic of an 'outstanding' lesson). I didn't always think that though.

Not that long ago I was dismissive of a speaker, partly because of what he was saying and partly because he had overrun and was now standing between me and my mid-morning coffee and cake. The message he was peddling and I was pooh-poohing:

'Within no more than five years there will be more support staff such as teaching assistants and learning mentors than there will be teachers in any school.'

I was wrong to be dismissive. That moment has arrived in many schools and, if it has not done so already, will arrive at your school very soon (despite the controversial debate as to whether teaching assistants are a cheap and effective solution or just a cheap solution to improving educational standards).

Either way, in light of the growth in teaching assistant numbers, it seems ironic that the effective use of teaching assistants (or higher level teaching assistants, connexions assistants or whatever else you may call them) is an area that seems to have been neglected by PGCE courses and appears only fleetingly on the NQT standards. What's more, effective use of teaching assistants rarely seems to feature in a school's self-evaluation of learning, other than as part of a sudden panic brought on by looking at the Ofsted criteria for effective lessons. Yet Ofsted clearly highlight the importance of teaching assistants when making their judgements about teaching and learning. Think about your last teaching assistant-supported lesson and decide where you fall in the following criteria:

- Outstanding – teaching assistants are well directed, with paired or joint teaching taking place; they reinforce and strongly support learning.

- Good – teaching assistants are well deployed and make a significant contribution.

- Satisfactory – teaching assistants are adequately managed and soundly contribute to pupils' learning.

- Unsatisfactory – teaching assistants provide an extra pair of hands, but minimal support for learning. They are poorly managed, lack knowledge/skills and contribute little.

Ofsted place a clear emphasis on teachers managing the work of teaching assistants in their lessons and contributing to the development of teaching assistants' skills and knowledge. So, you want to be seen in a good light by Ofsted? Sort out your teaching assistant. And if bowing to the grade criteria of an inspection regime is not enough to float your boat, just think how ludicrous it is not to get the very best for your students by using another professional in the room. In the Lazy Way, of course.

So, this chapter explores ways in which you can achieve outstanding practice with the help of your teaching assistant. So, it is time to stop thinking you are circumnavigating the curriculum on the Good Ship Learning with just you at the helm and start to use all those on board effectively, starting with teaching assistants.

I have listed ideas according to the amount of planning they may require, starting with the Lazy Teacher's favourite 'no planning'. After that there is 'a little bit of planning', in other words, time that can be snatched during one of your lazy lessons, followed by techniques that require 'some planning' but still no more than half an hour together over a coffee. Yet it is worth the effort for it is when you get to this last stage and invest that little bit of extra time that you truly see the benefits of using a teaching assistant the Lazy Way.

And if you think some of the ideas are a bit too obvious, just ask the teaching assistants in your school if they happen all the time. You may be surprised by what Mrs What's Her Name Again has to say ...

Lazy Ways to use the teaching assistant – activities with no planning

Meet and greet your teaching assistant every time

It is unlikely that a teaching assistant has just 'appeared from nowhere', as a teacher whom I was observing justified their non-use of a colleague. It may well be that you did miss that e-mail about the new student with impaired hearing joining your class. The student support won't have. So if you have a teaching assistant in the room, there is a good reason why. You might just want to say, 'Hello' and find out what that reason is. It could save your career.

Introduce and refer to teaching assistants by their name

Seems obvious, but how many times do you introduce teaching assistants to pupils by name and make it clear that the teacher and teaching assistant will be working as a team in your classroom? When you have inadvertently forgotten or, in some cases, do not know the name of your teaching assistant (and did not find out in the 'meet and greet'), give them an opportunity at the beginning of the lesson to introduce themselves to the class. And just a cautionary warning on this, it is better to do this straight away rather than face the embarrassment that I had of finding out the name of one of the teaching assistants that I worked with at a parents' evening. I am still mortified.

Communicate learning outcomes with the teaching assistant

You may not have the opportunity of joint planning time with your teaching assistant but this does not stop you having a chat with them as students are arriving. This gives opportunities for your teaching assistant to have confidence when dealing with the students as they can clarify and confirm what you have said. Remember, if students detect that the teaching assistant can help, that means fewer people wanting a piece of your time. If you want a bit of fun you can always give them the hospital pass and announce without any warning that Mrs Ferris would like to explain causes of desertification in the Sahel or irregular preterite French verbs. After all, you want to keep your second-in-command on their toes!

Get the teaching assistant to explain their role

When you are introducing the learning activities make it clear to the students what role the teaching assistant is going to play. When you do explain the role to the class, do it in such a way that, although hearing it for the first time the teaching assistant is able to get their instructions at the same time. Make sure that the teaching assistant role covers assessment, feedback and praise. Students soon latch on to who can sign off work as finished and will always go looking for that person.

Get private *and* public feedback from your teaching assistant

Your teaching assistant can feed back on all aspects of learning in the lesson. Use them to give you an insight into the behaviours, learning and ethos of the group, as it is likely they will have seen these students in more environments than you have. That includes how the students *and* you are doing! Ask publicly about the progress of specific groups of students, including groups that may have students assigned to your teaching assistant. In doing this you are giving your teaching assistant enhanced status in the classroom which will enable them to contribute more to the learning experience.

And if you have not done so as part of your end of session whole-class reflection on the lesson, remember to say 'thank you' before they leave. The Lazy Way is all about little things that make a big difference.

Lazy Activities with a little bit of planning

Could you just ...

Use the opportunity to look at your lesson plan to see what tasks the teaching assistant would be happy to lead. Perhaps collating answers on the board while you have a greater presence around the room? Working with a group of the most able while you take responsibility for those with additional needs during the discussion part of the lesson? Perhaps they could check to see if homework has been completed, thus avoiding the messy confrontation at the end. Students talk to teaching assistants with far less emotion and intensity over such issues as they perceive that telling them the truth will not result in as much trouble as if they tell you. Try it!

Given appropriate guidance, perhaps they could be a useful ally to reduce your marking burden? By doing any of these, you are clearly involving the teaching assistant in the learning process and, in turn, perhaps making their experience more enjoyable and fulfilling as well.

What feedback do you need?

Make it clear to the teaching assistant what formal feedback you may require from them to assist you not only with your own professional development but also concerning your legal responsibilities when it comes to providing evidence about students in your care. Teaching assistants can gather evidence on progression, behaviours, misconceptions, achievements and even those funnier moments that make it all worthwhile. Give them a Flip camera to record evidence that they can share with the class at the end. Either way, you should not be racking your brains about what to say when it comes to report time, annual reviews and parents' evenings.

What can your teaching assistant bring to the party?

Liaise with your teaching assistant over their experiences with the students in different seating plans, room layouts and learning activities. They often know pupils very well and can offer invaluable insights. If they are there for a specific student or group of students ask them how other staff deal with these additional needs and what advice they can offer.

Perhaps most importantly ask them what skills, interests, passions and talents they have as an individual. It seems a shame to waste them. I recently spent some time with a class who had to design a marketing campaign to promote learning. The teaching assistant was innocently helping the teacher fulfil the unsatisfactory Ofsted criteria by happily going around being just an extra pair of hands, when a student asked her for some help. It transpires that she was, in fact, a graphic design artist who runs her own business outside of school. To this day I bet the teacher of that class does not know that. What impact might a five-minute conversation between the teacher and the teaching assistant have had on that lesson?

What would you like to do? How can we help you do it?

Every school will claim they have an emphasis on continuing professional development in their school development plan. Yet how many can claim that it focuses on giving teaching assistants the

confidence and the skills that actually make a difference? What would you like to do? How can we help you do it? These are the two questions that should be asked of your teaching assistants.

A snatched five-minute conversation in a lesson may uncover someone with huge untapped talent who wishes to teach small groups or even the whole class. With your support they can do it. If you add together the current economic climate, which is seeing some very able and talented people consider becoming a teaching assistant as a way onto oversubscribed PGCE courses, we are on track to have the most talented teaching assistant force we have ever had.

Which begs a slight twist on the Cadbury Creme Egg question: How are you using yours?

Lazy Activities with some planning (but not enough to spoil your Sundays)

Look ahead in your scheme of learning

Do you need a teaching assistant in every lesson that you have been allocated one? Of course, the answer is yes! But do they need to be in the room? In providing planning time teaching assistants can prepare materials and resources, create movie and music clips for the lesson or generate differentiated resources from ones you have already. Always be thinking ahead as to how they will contribute to the learning in your lesson.

Subject toolkit

Provide your teaching assistant with a toolkit for a unit of work so they are not trying to help you with one hand tied behind their back – a scheme of learning, key words, glossary, a copy of the resources and any other useful documentation. It is unlikely they will have subject knowledge so these documents will enable them to access the learning. Ideally the documents should all be electronic to enable the teaching assistant to make amendments and new resources for you and the students. After all, if the teaching assistant needs the big picture of what is happening, don't the students?

Once you have assembled all these lovely, new differentiated resources insist that colleagues look at them at the next team meeting so they too see the benefit of moving beyond the teaching assistant job description that lists them as being an extra pair of hands.

Teaching assistant wish list

If you are not in a situation to have a teaching assistant attached to you personally or to your team, create a wish list of what work needs to happen to enhance learning for your students. Far from being pushy, your special educational needs coordinator will welcome the guidance in where they should place teaching assistants. It is far better to take responsibility than to have a year of rumbling discontent with the quality of in-class support your teaching assistant is providing.

Arriving at the Ofsted vision where your teaching assistants are 'well directed, with paired or joint teaching taking place, reinforcing and strongly supporting learning' is not the laziest of tasks. Yet neither, when tackled in this way, is it the most onerous.

The speaker who stood between me and my coffee and cake was right. There! I've said it. The effective use of teaching assistants is crucial if we are to meet the demands of a relevant and twenty-first century-proof education. Which can only mean if Mrs Didn't I See You in the Staffroom the Other Day is going to jump on board, it's time to snatch five minutes with her sooner rather than later.

Chapter 11
THE LAZY TUTOR

Chapter 11
The Lazy Tutor

If truth be known, tutor time is one of my favourite parts of the school day. Problems get solved, fun can be had and real characters emerge. How? By following the Lazy Way. Simply use the resource sitting there yawning in front of you, namely the students.

Now, there may be things you have to – or are supposed to – cover, such as the weekly slot for silent reading, as the English department has another go at whole-school literacy. Although, in my experience, this usually goes something like:

'Toby, just why do you think *that* reading material
is suitable for silent reading?'

'Because, Sir, you really would not want
me to read it out loud.'

Followed by whole-class laughter, me remarking how being smart is not a value we are working on this month and then the bell signalling the end of another 'silent' reading session during which the group has bonded, but not for the reasons the English department had in mind.

In contrast, the true Lazy Teacher sees this time each day as a real opportunity to get the most from the group but free from the shackles and restrictions of any planning.

For example, simply ask them: 'What don't you know that you would like to know?'

That one question, followed by getting them to find out the answers to their own questions, has led to some amazing sessions.

By doing this activity in tutor time as opposed to lesson time (where, by the way, it works just as well) I have found you need a little less forgiveness when the head teacher walks in and you are discussing why, if the black box flight recorder is never damaged during a plane crash, isn't the whole airplane made out of that stuff? Or can a fly without wings walk? (I seem to remember we had a wings theme going on due to the latest Red Bull advertising campaign.)

It is the sense of spontaneous discovery in activities such as this that makes them fun and memorable. I know because whilst I would perhaps like their year book comments to talk about their greater educational achievements, I am secretly very proud that my former tutees mention tutor time as one of their school highlights.

So, relax, trust your tutor group and my ex-tutees who came up with many of these ideas and propel your tutor time into the outstanding category – doing it the Lazy Way of course.

Magical Mondays

Magical Mondays started off because one member of my tutor group said he had seen an amazing trick down the pub (don't ask!). It was a genuinely impressive coin trick, even though it cost me 50p, and led to another student saying he could do a trick involving matches and someone else declaring they wanted to learn magic because it was 'Really cool with the girls!'

In my teachery way, I also saw it as a perfect opportunity for helping my students understand what great learners they really were. So, it became something of a tradition that, on Mondays, when we needed some magic to start the week, one of the tutor group performed a trick before huddles of interested people, rehearsing sleight of hand techniques or the latest 'pub trick' they had seen on the web or, in Matt's case, down the pub. Mondays became magical. Magical and lazy – what a brilliant start to the week.

I am going to tell you about ...

I was once asked at interview what my passion was. It is a surprisingly difficult question in fact and not because of any legal issues. When I returned to my tutor group and they asked how the interview went I put the question to them to see how they would respond. I was bowled over by the variety of responses and the surprises that this simple question threw up. The meekest, mildest member was into heavy rock and ended up trying to convince me of her love of music by lending me CDs. Another was a UK sailing champion with an unrivalled knowledge of knots and the coastline round the South West. The list goes on. The 'tell you about' sessions started off with students simply sharing their passions but ended up with people taking up new hobbies and learning other people's passions. And if school is not about that, what is it about?

I have a dream

Although I have no scientific evidence to back this up, I am convinced that the benefits of dreaming are undervalued in school. Not dreamy dreaming, floating away on puffy pink clouds to the world of sleep dreaming, but dreaming in the sense of letting yourself believe in what you want to do; what you want to achieve and what you are going to do to help you get it. The mental imagery you generate with such dreaming is very powerful. I believe that by sharing that dream with someone else it makes that commitment even stronger, as you are verbalising your images and answering questions about them which, in turn, makes them stronger.

In this activity, students share what it is they dream about for themselves. This can be built up from one-to-ones with you, to small group work to, finally, whole-class discussions. As well as building up trust and respect in the group, getting to know people's innermost thoughts and ambitions means you get to know that individual exceptionally well. I do not 'know' a tutor group until I know what they dream of for themselves.

And it is the 'themselves' bit that is important here. World peace, an end to animal testing and saving whales are all admirable, but deflect their thinking from what it *should* be – what do they really want for themselves? They might want to play a role in achieving world peace, ending animal testing or saving the whale, but what, specifically would that role be? And if they say, 'Being a protester', you might like to gently remind them that thus far, protesters have not brought about the change they are seeking.

DJ put the record on

This was created by the students who were growing increasingly bemused by my musical tastes. They quite rightly questioned me on why I liked the music I was playing so I challenged them why they like their music? 'DJ put the record on' was a result of that conversation. Students take it in turn to choose the (legally-sourced) music in tutor time for the week but can only play it once they deliver a presentation on the musicians involved, the musicians' influences and why they like this type of music.

When in six weeks you go on a musical journey that takes in American gangster rap (we referred to the gangs as 'teams' to fit in with school policy on gangs), to Lloyd Webber musicals, to Motown, then you know you are doing your bit to allow them to express themselves as well as covering half of the music curriculum!

It is this freedom of expression coupled with wanting to take an interest in their musical tastes which helps build yet more bonds with and within the group. What's more, I get legally sourced copies of the music to use in my lessons. 'DJ put the record on' is a truly lazy way of bonding with your group, getting great up-to-

date music to use in your lessons and having a musical lift during the day.

However, after one particularly graphic incident, I no longer advocate extending this to include music videos ...

Celebration Fridays

Just like knowing it is Friday because the canteen is serving chips, I wanted everyone to know it was Friday in tutor time. So we always celebrated something - anything - we had achieved over the past seven days. All types of success are included: individual, group, school team and whole school success, not to mention tutor group success. I always shared with the group what experience they have given me during the week to help them reflect on their actions.

It can take a while for them to build up the confidence to talk about success, so you may need to tip off some people to get the ball rolling but once you start there is no looking back. Encourage everything to be celebrated - from family birthdays, to swimming badges, to little brothers and sisters being born. Also have a focus on learning. Getting people to talk about their successes with learning over the last thirty hours of education is very powerful. Ever worried why parents' evening conversations can be hard work? It is simply because we do not engage students in conversations about learning often enough.

This is a great way to end the week and if you can find the time to phone home and carry on the celebration, it is a very lazy way of going into the weekend feeling oh so good about what you do!

On your way to work

Especially good if you have a tutor time in the morning - simply ask anyone you can (and I mean anyone) to pop in 'on your way to work' and say what they do for a living (or used to do). Reassure them that it's just a ten minute slot for a quick chat and a bit of Q&A and you'll be amazed who will drop by. My local zoo even sent someone! And in true lazy style, make sure you ask your tutor group if they could get anyone to come in. Why should you do all the work — it is their tutor time as well.

Conspiracy creation

Did we ever land on the moon? Did Elvis Presley ever die? Was Michael Jackson really in that coffin? Who is the 'war on terror' between? Are advertisers honest? Unpicking major events and beginning to develop probing and challenging questioning skills with students is crucial for all ages. You can often support your work with resources on YouTube, for example – but watch before showing. Students enjoy exploring and asking questions about these events to the extent that this activity can fill many tutor sessions.

Thinking time

Based on Radio 4's popular show *The Moral Maze* and the approaches advocated by the Philosophy for Children movement, pose difficult questions and allow discussion as a class:

When are you ever you?

When is it good to be you?

Is it ever right to wrong?

Is daring a good attribute?

Should you ever kill anything?

Ask students to pose the questions and chair the sessions. What they want to talk about is fascinating. I have even managed to help a student catch up on their GCSE coursework they were struggling with/refusing to do by secretly recording their presentation in tutor time. I am not sure who was most relieved: me for getting away with being sneaky, the English teacher for getting the work in or the student for overcoming what had become quite a contentious battleground with their English teacher.

Number puzzles

Here is a logic test. Many newspapers now print daily mathematical problems including Sudoku. Many schools have newspapers delivered. Yet why do many schools throw away (sorry, recycle) this daily resource? Only you will know the answer for your school but it does baffle me when this happens. Someone is making a daily resource for you but it gets thrown away. Madness to someone aspiring to be lazy. If the cutbacks mean you have to get your own copy of the *Guardian* jobs page so be it, but bring in your own puzzles. Better still, create a 'puzzle monitor' to bring them in for you. Students can take it in turns to set, mark and be in charge of the quiz.

Connect 4 championship

Should bringing board games to school really be confined to wet play or the last day of term at primary school? You can have hours of lazy but productive fun playing with Connect 4, which I have found to be a very inclusive game. Ask your students to bring in sets of this game and get them to run a championship over the course of two weeks. To make sure you get through all your games set a time limit on each game and sit back and watch the incredible competition and sense of purpose in the group. You will instantly improve punctuality and attendance in these two weeks as well as hitting the Personal, Learning and Thinking Skills full on. An outstanding tutor time? It is guaranteed!

Limericks

One of my early tutor groups that I inherited when I moved to a school inadvertently developed a love of poems, mostly funny ones it has to be said, after I shamelessly fooled an Ofsted inspector. Stumbling across a book of poems at a car boot sale prior to the Ofsted inspection (back in the days when you were given weeks, if not months of notice), I had a premonition that it would be useful. The premonition was soon realised when, as the inspector walked in on Monday morning tutor time, I calmly reached for the book and said to the class: 'And, as ever, 10JS, let's start the week with a poem.'

Having never read one to the group before, there was a sense of bemused anticipation but, being the wonderful group they were, a round of applause followed the end of the poem followed by much stifled laughter as the inspector (with an English and literacy brief) said how lucky the group were to start every week that way.

After that I felt morally obliged to carry on. I did and it was not long before, being a lazy tutor, I pushed the emphasis onto them to read and eventually write poems. These poems, or more accurately limericks, were often a satirical look at the week's events and not only showed great language skills but also the ability to push the boundaries as far as possible without causing offence.

As ever, by being lazy and demanding more from the students, you get far more out of tutor time than you ever could have hoped for. Let the students plan, deliver and respond to their own tutor time within the structure you provide them. And as for all those little tasks that still need doing, it goes without saying that the students all have various jobs on rotation, from looking after the plants, updating the notice board, checking planners for merits and signatures and taking the message file back. All of this frees you up to be the valuable, supportive, caring tutor that every student needs – all thanks to the Lazy Way.

Final Lazy Thoughts

The Lazy Way is here to stay.

This is not meant to be a catchy rallying call or a strap line for you to chant when all around you are rebelling and demanding that the photocopier is turned on again or your departmental colleagues wish to spend the next three years capitation on a set of books that will help the teacher teach but not the learners learn.

For me, saying that the Lazy Way is here to stay is a statement of fact.

The response of teachers whom I have canvassed during the course of writing this book all seemed initially shocked that I was going to advocate that we need to teach less. Yet to their credit, shock was unanimously replaced with a sense of excitement when they realised what the Lazy Way could actually mean for them: an end to the very things they hated about their jobs, which, coincidentally, often matched what students disliked about their learning.

So with this win-win scenario in place, there seems to be no reason why the Lazy Way should not make a difference in your classroom.

And if you are training to join the profession, can I make a bold suggestion: simply avoid the challenge of learning then unlearning an approach to teaching that advocates working all the hours possible. You will be exhausted, demoralised and end up full of regrets and seeking a career in, well, whatever you can, just to get out of teaching.

With this in mind and regardless of how long you have been teaching, now is the time to use this book to take on the challenge of following the Lazy Way. It will mean you are on your way to reaping the benefits of being a Lazy Teacher and your students are on their way to getting what they deserve – an opportunity to learn, not to be taught.

www.lazyteacher.co.uk

Bibliography

Canfield, J. and Wells, H. C. (1976) *100 Ways to Enhance Self-concept in the Classroom*, Prentice Hall, London.

Canter, L. and Canter, M. (1990) *Assertive Discipline: A Take-Charge Approach for Today's Educator (How's the discipline in your classroom)*, Lee Canter Associates, L.A.

Cowley, S. (2006) *Getting the Buggers to Behave*, Network Continuum Education, London.

Curran, A. (2008) *The Little Book of Big Stuff About the Brain*, Crown House Publishing, Carmarthen.

Davies, W., Frude, N. and Parker, T. (1993) *Preventing Face-to-face Violence: Dealing with Anger and Aggression at Work*, Association for Psychological Therapies, Leicester.

Department for Children, Schools and Families (2007) *Creating a Progress Culture*, Secondary National Strategies, DCSF, London.

Faupel, A., Herrick, E. and Sharp, P. (1998) *Anger Management: A Practical Guide for Teachers, Parents and Carers*, David Fulton Publishers, London.

Galvin, P. (1999) *Behaviour and Discipline in Schools: Practical, Positive and Creative Strategies for the Classroom Vol 2 (Behavior and Discipline in Schools)*, David Fulton Publishers, London.

Gilbert, I. (2007) *The Little Book of Thunks*, Crown House Publishing, Carmarthen.

Gilmore, J. (1994) *Enhancing Self-esteem*, Links Educational Publications, Shropshire.

Hughes, M. and Vass, A. (2001) *Strategies for Closing the Learning Gap*, Network Continuum Education, London.

Jackson, N. (2009) *The Little Book of Music for the Classroom*, Crown House Publishing, Carmarthen.

Keeling, D. (2009) *Rocket Up Your Class!,* Crown House Publishing, Carmarthen.

Long, R. (1990) *The Art of Self-esteem,* Nasen Publications, Tamworth.

Long, R. (1999) *Challenging Confrontation,* Nasen Publications, Tamworth.

Long, R. (1999) *Supporting Pupils with Emotional Difficulties: Creating a Caring Environment for All,* David Fulton Publishers, London.

Montgomery, D. (1990) *Managing Behaviour Problems,* Hodder and Stoughton, London.

Robertson, L. and Lawton, D. (1989) *Effective Classroom Control: Understanding Teacher-Pupil Relationship*s, Hodder and Stoughton, London.

Rogers, B. (1990) *You Know the Fair Rule: Strategies for Making the Hard Job of Discipline in Schools Easier*, FT Prentice Hall, London.

Ryan, W. (2008) *Leadership With a Moral Purpose,* Crown House Publishing, Carmarthen.

Bringing together some of the most innovative practitioners working in education today. www.independentthinkingpress.com

The Little Book of Bereavement for Schools — Ian Gilbert
ISBN 978-184590464-7

Dancing About Architecture — Phil Beadle Edited by Ian Gilbert
ISBN: 978-184590725-9

Where will I do my pineapples? — Gill Kelly Edited by Ian Gilbert
ISBN: 978-184590696-2

Oops!: Helping children learn accidentally
— Hywel Roberts Edited by Ian Gilbert
ISBN: 978-178135009-6

The Perfect Ofsted Inspection — Jackie Beere Edited by Ian Gilbert
ISBN: 978-178135000-3

Independent Thinking — Ian Gilbert
ISBN 978-178135055-3

Thinking Allowed — Mick Waters
ISBN 978-178135056-0

The Discipline Coach: Powerful, practical strategies for helping your students get the best out of themselves — Jim Roberson Edited by Ian Gilbert
ISBN 978-178135005-8

The Little Book of Awe and Wonder : A Cabinet of Curiosities
— Dr Matthew McFall
ISBN 978-178135001-0

The Philosophy Shop: Ideas, activities and questions to get people, young and old, thinking philosophically — Peter Worley and The Philosophy Foundation
ISBN 978-178135049-2

My School Improvement Doodle Book — Ben Keeling
ISBN 978-1-78135-051-5

The Little Book of Laughter for the Classroom and Staffroom
— Dave Keeling and Stephanie Davies
ISBN 978-178135008-9

www.independentthinkingpress.com

Bringing together some of the most innovative practitioners working in education today. www.independentthinkingpress.com

The Perfect Teacher Coach — Jackie Beere and Terri Broughton
ISBN 978-178135003-4

Perfect Assessment for Learning — Claire Gadsby Edited by Jackie Beere
ISBN 978-178135002-7

The Perfect Ofsted English Lesson — David Didau Edited by Jackie Beere
ISBN 978-178135052-2

Boring, Irrelevant and Hard: How to develop outstanding maths lessons that aren't any of the above — Ian Taylor
ISBN 978-178135050-8

Brave Heads: How to lead your school without selling your soul
— Dave Harris Edited by Ian Gilbert
ISBN 978-178135048-5

Trivium 21st Century: Preparing young people for the future with lessons from the past — Martin Robinson Edited by Ian Gilbert
ISBN 978-178135054-6

Full on Learning: Involve me and I'll understand
— Zoë Elder Edited by Ian Gilbert
ISBN 978-184590681-8

Altogether Now ... The Ultimate Plenary Book — Phil Beadle
ISBN 978-178135053-9

The Twenty-first Century Assembly Book — Will Ryan
ISBN 978-178135007-2

The Little Book of Dyslexia: Both sides of the classroom
— Joe Beech Edited by Ian Gilbert
ISBN 978-178135010-2

The Perfect Ofsted Lesson: Revised and Updated
— Jackie Beere Edited by Ian Gilbert
ISBN 978-178135088-1

www.independentthinkingpress.com